MW01516045

Finishing Year

Bentley Bryce Finley

Copyright © Bentley Bryce Finley 2014
All rights reserved. No part of this publication may be reproduced, stored in a retrieval system, or transmitted, in any form or by any means, without the prior written permission of the author, nor be otherwise circulated in any form of binding or cover other than that in which it is published and without a similar condition being imposed on the purchaser.

ISBN-13: 978-1502474674
ISBN-10: 1502474670

www.finishingyear.com
www.bentleybrycefinley.com

Questionable Quotes

"This Bryce Finley is the best writer on love, loss, and travel that Woody Allen, Peter Mayle, and Frances Mayes – combined – have never heard of."

"There has always been a hard way to get an education, and a long way, and now this author has found a way to combine the two."

"A little bit of *Beat the Clock* meets *What's My Line?* except, at the end, you are still wondering what this guy will do for a living."

"Funny." – Bryce

"Brave." – Lynne

"Who is this guy?" – Rachel

Reliable Quotations

"Men are not born, but fashioned." – Desiderius Erasmus

"Cometh the hour, cometh the man." – English cricketer Cliff Gladwin (about himself), in a Derbyshire and England test match against South Africa, at Durban, Dec. 20, 1948.

"And the hour... produced the man." – P.G. Wodehouse, *Aunts Aren't Gentlemen* (1974).

A Grand Tour

Sometimes you just have to go and do what you have to go and do. We have all heard that gem in one of its various forms. I like to include the 'go' part when I say it, because that is what I usually do: I go. I don't know who first offered up this ambiguous little piece of advice, but I hope it was a very smart man who just happened to be traversing a difficult patch or awkward moment (perhaps middle age or unwanted hair loss) and that everything eventually worked out for the best, because I have just gone and taken his very stupid advice.

Don't get me wrong. Nobody can argue with the basic validity of the saying, it was just never intended for you to act upon. But, as I say, the saying itself holds water. Its merit seems unassailable. When people bring it up in conjunction with some dark task or dreaded duty that they must, however grudgingly, perform, they invoke the phrase simply as a way of steeling themselves, of gaining courage in the face of the inevitable.

Such a person, looking down the barrel of a tough chore or dirty, distasteful job, can put their self-interest or weak stomach aside and tell themselves that, well, yes, a man's gotta do what a man's gotta do, and then they can get on with it.

But there is an opposite side, and my case falls on that other side. Mine is the story of what happens when the saying is used – some would say fine-tuned and then bandied about – in the interest of raw self-indulgence, personal goal reaching, or anything along those lines that doesn't really excite an innocent bystander or third party.

In this second instance, the saying is usually used as a

means of deflecting criticism levelled against one's person, or of mitigating feelings of guilt in that person, or the largely counterproductive placement of blame upon that person, as, for example, when one goes and drops a hundred grand on a completely unnecessary but highly appealing sports car. Onlookers don't always stand up and cheer this brand of behaviour. This kind of activity can be seen as taking away from the heroism of the earlier-mentioned, fatalist application of the saying that most people feel trapped into fulfilling, where a person selflessly does what must be done.

But the saying applies equally well to both operations: it holds true when we are morally duty bound to do something, as well as when we simply want to do something. In the second case (where we already know I find myself), one just feels the pull of a certain "I don't know what," and one just has to go and do what one has to go and do. There is no other remedy for it.

This leads to questions. Is that course acceptable? Is it selfish? Is it both? It is probably both. I say probably, because I am having a worry moment about it right now.

I have decided to set off on a journey – a voyage of discovery, of sorts – at a time when my journeying should be done, my voyaging should be reserved to 5-star hotels, and whatever I need to discover should have been discovered by now. But this journey is something that I feel I just have to go and do. There is no proof whatsoever that this is something that I really must do. At least, there is no external, physical proof. It is just something I feel.

Having actual proof would be different. Then there would be absolutely no question. You need to do it? Alright then, go ahead and do it. But that would be the first approach again, the old master-slave, boss-employee, you-and-your-mortgage-banker kind of 'must' that people have known since the beginning of time, or at least of mortgage banking.

There is a world of difference between a 'must' you can

see and a 'must' that is technically invisible. There is the clear and present danger of the 'must' directed at you, and then there is the touchy-feely, sensitive-guy, only-you-and-your-God kind of 'must' that is internally directed and could only be put into words if your stomach could speak. That is the kind of have-to-do feeling I am experiencing.

That second way is the way you apply the 'man's gotta do' schtick when you go off to do something that only your heart is telling you to do, while your head and most of your acquaintances or internal organs are screaming at you to throw on the brakes. It is the exact opposite of how most of society, your co-workers, your partner, and your pocketbook hope you will behave.

It does make me wonder which one of the two meanings the originator of the phrase really had in mind: the follow your brain, tried-and-true school of doing necessary evils, or the romantic dreamer, fiddle-while-Rome-burns (researchers say that probably never happened) method of getting what you really, really want. Maybe he meant both. I am not sure. One thing I am sure of is that if you apply the phrase the second way, somebody or some part of their being is not going to be happy with you.

Look at me. I have just set off on the path that leads to Door Number 2. I am a 48-year-old single father about to take a sort of gap year to finish my university education as an international exchange student in Europe. It seems like my only chance of finishing a long-delayed (and first) university degree, in art history. To top it all off, I live in North America. I have spent my life without a university degree, and now I have gone back to school to study a subject that would be better served by learning it half way around the globe, where art actually lives.

Given only that little bit of information, it sounds perfectly reasonable that, if a foreign university were willing to give me a small scholarship to go to Europe and study art, I should take them up on the offer, shouldn't I? It sounds grown up and responsible to be finishing something long left undone, like completing a lingering project that has taken over your office, desk, garage, or basement.

Finishing my degree will change my life, won't it? It will show my almost grown kids (one of whom has already dropped out of high school) that education – and finishing things – is important. I can change the stars.

If you consider for a moment that the subject of my studies is art history and that I have so far been studying this topic at university in Canada (a young country without the rich artistic traditions and collections of Europe), then it would seem to make even more sense to be able to stop squinting at the tiny reproductions in my textbooks and haul myself off to Europe for a couple of semesters to finish this degree in the world's single most important storehouse of art. There I could see many of the world's greatest masterpieces firsthand, and all within a few days' travel of each other. Right? Well, I can assure you, not everybody sees it that way, and at times, I am not even sure I do.

I am, as I said, having a worry moment right now. I have just set off on this clearly sensible (see above) but elective path, and even I am having doubts about it. Like elective surgery, which one can almost casually decide to go in for by seeing a billboard or while chatting over coffee with a friend and noticing a bit of a wobble above her elbow, it is still surgery and should not be taken lightly.

And then there are the costs to think about. What did I have to do to get here? What has it already cost me, and what is it likely to still cost me in the future? I had to break up with my girlfriend in order to be free enough to even make the decision to come here. I had to pawn my last kid off onto his mother, so that he could finish high school at home while I finished my last year of university overseas. I had to give stuff away, throw things out, hand a car over to my oldest child, and put everything else into storage.

When I go home, I have no idea what I will do (I am

studying art, for Pete's sake) or what I will go back to or even exactly where home will be. I don't have a house or apartment waiting, and I will likely still be, in truth, one or two courses short of having my degree at the end of this exchange, so there won't be any new opportunities waiting for me as a result.

At least monetarily, this adventure seems to have already cost me more than I could ever possibly hope to recoup from it. But that is also the good part. This thing I've gotta do clearly isn't about finances. It isn't so simply self-serving as that. It is about love, the love of art, and it is about the art of living and doing something you really feel compelled to do. And it is about Europe and that voyage of discovery.

In a sense, I am embarking on a very un-grand tour of Europe, a poor substitute for the proper Grand Tour that upper-class, young, English nobles took to discover the Continent and its treasures a few centuries ago, or the well-financed and well-supported kind of gap-year modern students take when they come from well-heeled homes.

Even under the best conditions, many people who set off on such a Grand Tour or gap year probably felt the same fear or trepidation I do. The richer ones who undertook that original Grand Tour of Europe three or four centuries ago must have hated the bumpy tracks that led from city to city, the incoherent babble of foreign tongues, the dust, dirt, poor accommodations and strange foods of a hundred different towns, the exorbitant cost of carriage repairs, and the general sparseness of ATM machines.

Modern gap-year tourists – the latter-day voyagers, the middle-educated sons and daughters of the upper-middle class, the wanderers, hippies, college students, and druggies – have always equally despised the feeling of riding crowded buses on marathon journeys and waking up broke in places like Afghanistan with nothing but a burned spoon, a throbbing headache, and the vague feeling that they originally came to this place with a backpack.

It is funny how the two are so similar. The Grand Tour was meant to be (usually) a once-in-a-lifetime trip-cum-education for a wealthy young Englishman. A gap year, on the other hand, was pretty much the exact opposite: a year off from work or study for the (largely) educated but occasionally broke offspring of a decidedly lower class. What I am now doing lies somewhere in between. My year will really amount to more of a finishing year, something once popular for young girls on their way to womanhood, sent to finish their last year of formal education at private boarding schools, largely in Switzerland.

So taken altogether, but leaving out the parts about being wealthy, drugged out in Afghanistan, or a young woman in Switzerland, you pretty much have a picture of what I am doing.

It really is a Grand Tour, at least in its intention. A Grand Tour was aimed at finishing a young man's education by exposing him to the arts, cultures, and original sources of the surprisingly deep classical Greek and Roman underpinnings of our Western civilization. This was done through an extended and expensive land tour of the European continent.

Lots of people have gone on the Grand Tour. Their names largely escape us now, but many of them wrote detailed accounts of their trips. Fictional ones, ironically, come most easily to mind (Scarlett O'Hara's original love interest, the Ashley Wilkes character, from *Gone With the Wind*, is two years home from a three-year Grand Tour near the beginning of the book). Going on a Grand Tour was quite the thing to do for a rich young man, especially one from Britain. And doesn't it sound like it had such noble intentions, to look at the art and experience first-hand all that the various cultures of Europe had to offer? Paradoxically, what propelled most of those rich young Englishmen (and later, newly rich Americans) outward into the world was not their general love of art and culture (or even adventure or the unknown) but rather the unchecked greed of their elders and the veritable serfdom of most other people in the British Isles and America, backed up by an almost complete lack of equitable property laws and basic human rights that allowed their families to exploit enough people and resources to amass the vast fortunes that supported such worthy undertakings. But I digress.

Be that as it may, the Grand Tour was an important part of upper-class life from about the 1660s until the advent of the railways and the coming of mass transportation and then the gap-year traveller, which pretty much ruined it for everybody.

But until then, intrepid young men ventured out into the wilds of Europe at great family expense to rediscover and experience the remains of the greatest art and cultures the world had ever known.

Later, because much of the Grand Tour focused on an appreciation and experiencing of the great works of art housed in the most enduring establishments of Europe, slightly more impoverished artists and architects of the time began to feel the call to make the trip. These poorer types had to do without the wisdom and guidance of the normal rich young man's personal guide or teacher (called the Cicerone or 'bear leader'). The less well-heeled made the trip easier and more affordable by hitting a limited number of stops in a more standard itinerary. This, of course, happened right around the time when travel agents were getting their start and led directly to the 24-cities-in-23-days school of travel everyone knows from today's packaged bus tour.

But before that, even the odd impoverished artist (provided he had the support of a wealthy patron or two) could go out and see the world and the great art in it and draw inspiration from hundreds and hundreds of years of earlier artists' work in the very places of their creation. After all, there was only so much artists could learn from the printed copies of distant works that circulated back in their home countries. Ancient ruins were another thing that creative types needed to see in their rocky reality. To obtain a full and true understanding of the masterpieces left strewn across the landscape of Europe by past generations of artists and architects, the young, aspiring artist had to go out and make, if not a Grand Tour, then at least a comprehensive un-grand tour, and that is now exactly what I find myself doing.

Aside from the worry, it feels good. After years of squinting at those tiny reproductions in textbooks, I have finally – like those generations of artists, art lovers, and cultural travellers before me – taken it upon myself to go and see these wonders with my own eyes and in person.

The Grand Tour never should really have gone out of fashion just because somebody invented the slide show or the overhead projector. I cannot believe that it is not a requirement of my degree to go and see a set number of the world's greatest artworks and drink in their splendour firsthand. Anyone who studies this and has half a chance to do so really must.

But it is hard. Even Sister Wendy, the famous art historian-nun who takes herself off to all the great art places and writes books or sends back television shows about them, has sponsors in the BBC. But watching someone else do it is a poor substitute for doing it yourself. You will never know really, exactly, entirely what a piece of art or a building looks like or how it makes you feel unless you go to it yourself. And if Sister Wendy can do it, so can you. Or at least you would think so.

Setting off on the Grand Tour was never an easy task. My brothers-in-art had to raise money, beg, borrow, plead, and steal, or sell things like bodily fluids to start them on their way. They had to rely on the kindness of family and friends and sometimes strangers. They had to find those elusive patrons, pack their belongings, leave the familiar shelter of home or studio, say farewell to model, lover, or muse, and gird themselves for a certain amount of uncertainty that even the possession of the most adequate emergency medical insurance could not assuage.

And I had to do the same thing. This is the price we must pay. There are just not enough travelling exhibitions of art in the entire world to bring enough artworks to our doorsteps for us to truly appreciate from the comfort of home. Much art can't even travel (although the Brits and the Germans have been known to pick up and bring back stunningly large objects, such as whole buildings or entire city streets, in their travels).

As concerns most art, however, we must travel to it. And there can only be one reason to do this: love. And, at least in this day and age, the simple act of doing something for love is sometimes subject to suspicion and even ridicule. What about your job? What about the future? This will put you behind, delay your progress, force you to change plans or shift priorities. There must be another way?

These arguments, you might notice, are all ruled by the head. The internal compass of the heart, if we even remember how to access it, enjoys little trust or recognition in today's world. Any move we make that excludes the brain (or the brains of those around us) or relegates it to the role of second opinion in these decisions brings it rushing back in to offer any last minute advice we might still be willing to listen to, just in case we missed it the first ten times around.

There is nothing so bothersome as a brain stuck on repeat or one you have just locked out of the house but now find incessantly scratching at the window with a sorry look on its face. All this hullaballoo does is offer the brain another chance to come slinking back in, and it usually does. It comes crawling back, begging for forgiveness, and offering its help so that we can then undertake the rational and serious business of soul searching, but this is a further ruse.

The thing about soul searching is that there is absolutely no reason to do it. If the purpose of soul searching is to find out what we think, well, we already know what we think. We think, in instances like this, that we are crazy or selfish or naive or some other black thought. If the purpose of soul searching is to know what we truly want or feel, well, then the same thing is true: we already know it.

Usually, that thing we want is whatever we are busy soul searching about. Should I buy that Porsche? On credit? Should I get that tummy tuck? Should I eat that last ice cream sandwich? We already know what we want or we wouldn't be thinking so hard about it. All soul searching does is run our desires through a complicated and unreliable filter of – get this – what *other people* want or what we think they might want. Basically, we take the temperature of other people's moods and sound the depths of our own guilt.

The only good part of soul searching is that soul searching makes us at least question if we have the strength not only to do what we propose but whether we can withstand the psychic pain that is surely headed our way if we don't conform to other people's ideas, if we don't bend our will to meet their expectations when what we propose does not meet with their approval. We surely already know that what we want will incur their wrath. That is a given. Soul searching asks us if we are strong enough to withstand the onslaught.

Instead of suffering through all the tossing and turning and sleepless nights of soul searching, why don't we instead just say, "Okay, world, this is what I want. I am ready. Unleash the Kraken." Then, have the Kraken heaped upon us and be done with it. Once the barrage of wrath (or Kraken) is over and we can once again feel our legs (assuming they are still there), we can start using them to get moving. Why not do that instead?

The answer is that we have been taught to try to please people, to try to make them happy, no matter how unhappy they might already be. What idiots we are! We can't make people happy, and somewhere along the line, we learned that. We don't, we won't, we never do make them happy. People decide completely on their own how they are going to feel about our actions and the resulting effects on them, and there is not one thing we can do about it. But no matter what, we try to run our decisions through this mill, simply out of the milk of human kindness, to see if we can somehow soften the blow, mitigate the effects, or manage the feelings of dread and disaster others will surely feel.

But if we already know what we want, the soul searching is useless. We could save all that gut-wrenching second guessing and move on more quickly to helping others see that our choices for ourselves are not choices against them, and that we are just doing our own job in this life, which is making sure that our own lives are ones we can be happy with. This is a much harder sell than it sounds.

Either way, or any way, I have decided to set off on my personal gap year, at whatever cost it will extract from me. Sometimes I feel that this year is less a year of discovery, like a Grand Tour might have been, and more a year in one of those Swiss boarding schools where those young women from a few generations ago studied mostly etiquette and the kind of life lessons nobody could make a living from. At most, that sort of finishing year promised to prepare people for nothing more than marriage. With a degree in art history, I feel sometimes that I am doing nothing more than setting myself up for a career as someone's husband. Conversely, that is part of the reason that sent me flying here in the first place.

Shall we now start at the beginning? Yes, alright, but briefly. This could require more explanation (read: apologies) later. I had been living in Victoria, British Columbia, Canada, for at least the past five or six years. I had come back to the city where I had spent some time as a child and where my ex-wife had moved with our kids so that she could go to school. When her course finished and she got a job out of town, the kids – two boys, about 15 and 11 at the time – wanted me to come and take over from her so that they could stay put.

I did that, and a short time later, found myself working at the local university, dating a professor, and slowly starting to take a few courses myself, with the goal of finishing my degree. When my contracted position ended three years later, I was still studying, but now full-time, and living with my girlfriend. Then, one spring, with about a year left to go in my degree (at the speed I was going) and no job at that moment, two things happened at nearly the same time: I experienced a profound lack of funds, and I discovered on my school's website an exchange opportunity to Europe that included a small scholarship equal to about two thirds of my tuition.

The idea of Europe, especially for studying art history, combined with the possibility of obtaining any kind of financial aid to study (my school had, up until that time, never given me a penny, and I was ineligible for student loans) started to work on my mind. At that moment, I had no other way of continuing my studies at home that would not have been even more of a burden than it already was. I still had one son at home, things to pay for, and no idea how to accomplish everything I wanted to do. Then this opportunity appeared. As small as it was, it stuck in my mind.

I decided to take some time to consider this exchange opportunity, but when I brought the idea up at home, it did not sit well with my girlfriend, and, well, why should it have? I would have been gone for at least one semester, quite long in the course of any relationship. But the more I thought about it, the less I could accept the idea of not even trying, and the more I thought about going, the more upset she became about it.

It seemed like the decision, or even considering the possibility, could only be undertaken in small steps. Everything would have to proceed one piece at a time, and then, if I was accepted, I could still make a decision. So I applied, and as luck would have it, my school (which has some 20,000 undergraduate students running around and could only send two students on this exchange) only had two people apply. If we passed a sort of short interview with the head of the German department, we would be accepted and could go, and I was.

Then, standing right in front of that new possibility, I did not feel that I could say no. It had been at least 11 years since I had set foot in Europe, roughly the same amount of time that I had been divorced from my German wife, the mother of my children. As a much younger person, and as the husband of a European, I had spent a lot of time in Europe as a photographer and visiting family. Later, I had gone there for work for high tech companies, but then my European connection and dreams (as a child, I had always dreamed of living there) ended.

A new sort of reality took over, and this one saw me collecting properties and cars in Canada, and generally building up a large supply of things that could never easily be shifted to a life overseas, and I slowly just forgot about the dream, until I saw that listing on my university website. Then, it started all over again. Life is like that.

To make the story simple, I decided to go. I had to leave my girlfriend and pack my stuff, give away at least one car, send that kid off to his mother, and go. In the end, I settled on going to Europe for two semesters (might as well get the full experience if I was going to cause so much havoc doing it). I would study German and art history at a university in Mannheim, Germany, and live in a dorm with my fellow students (all half my age, as usual) and – between classes or while on holidays – try to see the great art museums of Europe. I would also work part-time in the university's International Office, to supplement my savings. The school would pay most of my tuition, which was too bad, in a way (schooling in Germany is nearly free, but while on exchange, our home universities would continue to charge their usual fees, so the German scholarship would end up being eaten by our home universities and leave us nothing).

And in a strange twist of events, going overseas suddenly made me eligible for a handful of scholarships, bursaries, and financial incentives from my own school. I entered the competitions, wrote the essays, gathered the reference letters, and came away with the first financial support I had ever received from my home university, all to go away and study somewhere else.

All of this was thought up, arranged, and carried out in a few short months. This can create a path of destruction in your life, for sure, but a path that leaves the ground scorched and fertile for something new to grow in.

I am now a 48-year-old international exchange student living in Europe and studying the history of art. How did I ever get so lucky? Or, if you prefer, how did my life ever get so screwed up? Explaining that will require the long form.

Loves, Labours, Loss

I blame it on poor life choices.

Setting off on any kind of voyage of self-discovery such as this certainly gives cause and opportunity for a little self-refection. If that wasn't accomplished during all of the previous planning, preparation, or packing, it will be by the time you say goodbye to whomever comes to see you off at the airport, when you sit waiting for the plane to depart, when you are up in the air, when you land in your new home country, on the drive to your new place, or somewhere along there.

I tend to pack first and think later, so it was not until long after the exchange had been arranged, I had paid my housing fees and school deposit, and broken the news to everyone that mattered, that I paused to consider how all of this had happened to me, or how I had caused it to be.

How, for instance, does a person reach this age and still have his life so seemingly out of order? I say seemingly, because under the surface, it might be largely like I wanted or planned it to be, but to the outside world, it looks off.

I think I always intended to be rich by now, so going back to school should not have been an issue anyway, but I obviously didn't do the necessary things to make that so. I know people who did, plenty of them, but I never made it happen. Sure, a few of those people are as dumb as fence posts, but they had something outside themselves going for them, like luck, timing, wealthy parents, coincidence. They rarely used going back to school as a stepping stone to success.

I think I also thought that stability would find me somewhere along the way, but we evidently passed in the night and have not seen each other since. I never finished university the first time around, and I never much worked in the disciplines I studied after that. I started in one career and then another, and that keeps you the perpetual bottom boy in any field. I never followed one path to the end. When I did get somewhere, it was by learning enough and sticking for a while, but I would eventually change direction again, not recognizing that I had just been looking at the key to doing better.

A girlfriend called me a financial train wreck, but I am not that bad. I own things. I am strangely secure with what I have, but my income has admittedly been erratic, enough to buy a modestly priced Porsche or piece of land one day and little enough the next to rent a house that resembles a crystal meth lab, although in a very nice neighbourhood.

Where is the partner for life I thought I would have by now? True, I was married once (for 17 years) and have two children, but lately my relationships have been getting shorter and shorter, going from five years to three to two to one. Even the worst gambler could see the pattern here.

Likewise, where is the professor, doctor, or lawyer my mother always thought was lurking inside of me? You've got me there, too. My grades have always been good enough to do any of those things, but the will has never been strong. I did apply to the law school at my home university (but not at others, because my kids did not want to move), but my school turned me down twice: once they thought my application was not complete (they said they needed a copy of my high school diploma, although I had attended two universities already); the second time, they gave no reason at all (they take a small number of mature students with some university experience each year, and I was not one of those that year). But I happily took the news and ran with it.

That led me to the path I am now on, and it seems like a reasonable one, to a certain degree. Studying is a noble thing, but how does a person, at the age of 48, wind up being an undergraduate, still a year away from a cap and gown, instead of working on a second PhD? Well, first I went to university where I studied in a program that was not so good and not so affordable. Some people might say it was fine; others might say I was too young to know for certain, but even after all these years, I stand by the opinion. It was horrendously expensive, and after two years, I was so far in debt that my young mind could not see how I would ever pay it off (my banker saw: it would take exactly seven years, a quarter of my life when paid up).

That is a true story, but it still doesn't allay my fears as to how I ended up here. I was always a good student, so why didn't I stick? Even the worst post-grad would be done by now, have completed their studies, and be well on the way to making at least the first of many payments on their student loans. Others would be über-professors, über-doctors, or plain old personal injury lawyers by now. Where is my senior management position, my accounting designation, the advertising company I should have founded, the waterfront home complete with hand-built, wooden sailboat, my entire self-image?

I don't even practice my first profession (photography) or my second (journalism), and I realize now that I would be much further ahead in life if I had only stuck with one of those two, instead of doing the dozens and dozens of other things I variously undertook in the intervening years. This is not how I imagined my life would turn out. It is a sobering thought. I am still not sure what it all means.

The only thing I can say for certain is that if you are a 48-year-old undergraduate student, it is fairly certain that you are not on any of the various career paths you might have imagined yourself taking one day, when you were growing up and thinking about this stuff. That much is painfully clear. No school-aged kid says that what they want to be doing when they grow up is exactly the same thing they are doing right now, namely sitting on their butt in a classroom, going to school, listening to teachers, learning. If you ask them if they would consider still being at it when they are close to 50, you would get few positive answers. It just isn't done.

However, if you do find yourself still a student at this age, you can also take solace in the fact that you are actually one of the luckier ones. You are attempting – and getting the chance – to wipe clean a messy, incomplete slate and start anew. Another thing is true: if you can manage to do school at this age (and here I mean use your brain plus escape the ties of anything else holding you back), you are very lucky.

If you can pack up and fly off for a year-long overseas student exchange and see up close what you have thus far only seen in books, then you are truly blessed. Sure, it could mean you have no financial house to put in order, but it could also mean you have no debts or obligations that inextricably tether you. No partner, children, mortgage payment, or car loan is standing in your way, for better or worse. It means that whatever ties you had, no matter how strong they seemed to be at the time, could be stretched or broken in order for you to do this.

This might sound like you don't have much, yet it begs the question: how did you ever get so lucky? Early psychoanalysis would almost surely have pointed to your earliest childhood experiences. So much about where our lives first went off the rails is explained by (or blamed on) our upbringings, circumstances, finances, and those poor life choices I mentioned earlier.

So much of our daily lives involves simply glossing over the past that we often don't look back that far, but starting this story any later than that would be missing an opportunity to listen to the pent-up rantings of that delicate inner child inside all of us that is still upset about the loss of some favourite toy. That child is still searching for that toy, and to hear its precious but sometimes skewed wisdom (the wisdom we often still live by but never clearly hear in our rational, adult minds) might shed some light on how this all came to pass.

If I were to lie down right now on some analyst's couch, the effort would probably go a long way towards explaining the story of how, while you came to own a house, a job, a dog, 2.5 kids, and a minivan, I am living a spare student life in a spare student dorm halfway around the world, working on something you finished a quarter century ago (your university degree). I might think that it is the result of recent events, but it is probably more the result of my character, which was formed when I was young, long before any recent loves, labours, or losses.

How did that early childhood look? I am the product of a broken home, so to speak. Everyone grows up in one of these, really, and I include here homes in which the parents stayed together. Given that proviso, a broken home is really only cracked and does not set me apart from anyone else on the planet. It just means that some things don't work in our upbringing and not that everything has absolutely gone haywire. That would be a crack house or a crime scene.

The one or two things that were broken or cracked most significantly while I was growing up were probably professional and locational stability, two things you have probably noticed about me already, from the story so far. I am still suffering from both of them. In order not to blame anybody inappropriately, though, I should say "acting out" rather than "suffering from."

As concerns my future entry into the world of work (and it is still, amazingly, in the future), I cannot recall my parents ever addressing the issue when I was young. They never talked about professions or asked us (my one-year-older brother or my six-year-younger sister) what we might want to be when we grew up. I think I thought there was either not much need to consider this, because I would just go on the way I was forever (could I have been more right?), or that there was plenty of time to consider it later (could I ever have been more wrong?). And yet, here I am, still considering it.

But somewhere in the back of all of our mind's, we must have known that we would one day have to work, and the hand-me-down clothes we got from our older uncles should have been a clue that we would, indeed, have to work harder than the members of our family had done up until that time. But I am also pretty sure that nobody ever, ever said that we would have to decide what that future work would be. This was surely an oversight. The first I ever heard of this was on my graduation day from high school.

Graduation from high school is, of course, the day on which one of your parents' biggest dreams is about to be realized: they will be able to use your room for another purpose. For years you have basically been standing between your parents and a pool table or a den or a sewing room. So, on that day, after which I would wake up and no longer be a school kid, my father (long divorced from my mother and in no way connected with any future use of my room) leaned over to me at my graduation dinner table and said, "So, what are you going to do now?"

Indeed.

This was a question I had never been asked before, not even by my high school guidance counsellor. The question really floored me. What was I going to do? There was nothing for me in my small hometown, I knew that. At least in the short term, I knew I would leave home and head off to my brother's apartment in the big city for a few days before flying off to Europe to see the pen pal who had stayed with me the summer before (and who I would, in unrelated events, later marry and have two kids with).

But I knew that the fine point of the question had nothing to do with all of this. It had to do with work, and I had no answer for it. What would I do for work, once the few hundred dollars I had left after paying for my flight were gone? How did I want to earn a living from that day forward? Where was the money going to come from? And why, in the name of God, did nobody bring this up earlier? Probably they had never thought much about it, even for themselves.

My father was never really a sound role model in that department, although I feel I learned tons of other useful things through him. Besides, I myself had never really identified with any particular role model from the world of work. I don't think that, at least until Darth Vader came along in *Star Wars* that I had ever seen anyone who truly loved their work. Unhappily, though, Darth Vader was not my father. My father did a number of things in his working days, only about three of which I can even remember, and almost none of which (I am at least pretty sure) he ever cared much for. Seriously. Now contrast that with Mr. Vader.

My other immediate role models were similar. My mother and stepfather worked, but seeing them always short of money made me think that working a normal job was not going to be the answer to anything, either. A pay cheque seemed like more of a false promise than a valuable reward. I had an uncle who played a mean guitar but only worked at that on weekends, while I am pretty sure he could have made a career of it at one time. I played the drums in that same band and quite liked it, and while we earned money at it, neither of us took it up as a profession. My grandparents had operated a business but never passed it on to their kids, so it was sold out of the family, and nobody I can think of has been in business since.

None of this rubbed off on me exactly, not the business lessons, not the lesson of following your passion, none of it.

The next deficiency in my preparation involved location. As any expert in real estate will tell you, location is the key ingredient in success. I don't think anybody in my family ever gave a rat's ass about location. We never moved to anywhere that was 'in' or 'happening' or likely to boom any time soon. We moved simply for monetary reasons or to stay close to our roots or to get more space. Yet somehow we moved around like peas in a shell game. We went somewhere more affordable, more spacious, somewhere to get a job, but nowhere that something could be laid as a foundation and then built upon in the future. And we particularly liked to live far away from any university.

And now, years later, the cruel truth has come home to roost, and that truth is that nobody who had spent all that time building themselves a profession would have had to do all of that moving in the first place. Having a decent support system (like an education or your own business) built under you takes care of a lot of the little problems of life (like simply 'moving' somewhere to be 'better off'). Dentists settle down. They aren't friendly towards moving and meeting untold sets of new and strange teeth in order to grind out a living. Demand for travelling dentists has really dropped off in the last 100 or so years. My mother and stepfather did settle down for quite a long period, from the time I was in Grade 5 or 6 until I finished high school, but only in a tranquil, pretty place that didn't offer much more than the nature that surrounded it. And then I set off on a location/dislocation odyssey of my own design. All of that shifting from place to place must have settle in my bones.

It does make a person envy the relative stability of others, their still, unmoving lives. Strangely, I have no bad memories of all those abodes. Hardness only sets in when I think of all the places I moved to of my own accord. From the time I was 17, I lived in a laundry list of places, and true to my history, almost none of them were places that were in, happening, or likely to form a foundation for later personal growth or professional success.

The only ones worth mentioning are the truly strange: the travel trailer in my parent's backyard; the childhood bedroom of my future wife at my future in-laws' in

Germany (although my future wife had temporarily broken up with me at the time); the interior of my own van for a summer between years at university; our own first bought-and-paid-for home that had no doors, windows, water, electricity, sewer connection, or telephone when we first moved in.

In between and even after, we rented, owned, leased out, or bought more places.

Madness.

Not just locations changed. First I lived with my family (wife and children), then with a French girlfriend for five years in two houses that we bought, then alone, and on and on.

Professionally, life was similar. During all of those years, I was a jack-of-all-trades, if nothing else. True, I started out as a photographer and newspaper editor. I worked for the toughest, chainsmokingest, old-school newspaperman you could ever care to meet, and I would not have needed one more minute of training to enjoy a long and fruitful career in journalism, but I did not stick with it. I went off to university, hoping for a better life.

What I became was a film student, a stock photo agent, I studied watchmaking and French and woodworking and marketing and worked in copywriting and sales, and so on.

Somehow all those years passed in that fashion, not only in my working life, but in my relationships. They were all important to me, but my relationships were getting noticeably shorter with each successive mate. I thought maybe there was something I needed to change about myself in order keep going. Looking back, I figure the main thing about myself that I could have changed would have been to just stay put, stay calm, and tackle that lack of settling down and sticking with one thing.

That lack seemingly led to another: my apparent financial instability. Sure, part of that could have been due to my adventurous spirit, but it also could have been due to my failure to choose, study, and then stick with a chosen profession that would match the rather stable girls I was going out with. Either that or pick more unstable girls.

I tried a bit of both, actually, but eventually chose to accept that I did not like my finances, even if they were okay sometimes. This was not how I imagined my life would be at this point. I was not doing nearly as well as I would have thought by that time. I was, at times, not even doing as well as I personally had done in the past, and I was nowhere near the level of stability or comfort or accomplishment that I thought I would by now enjoy.

Probably everybody thinks this about their own lives at some point, no matter how well or how poorly they might be doing. Some of us only compare ourselves to our own better selves. Some of us compare ourselves ceaselessly to others. But in the end, you simply decide how you feel about your life's progress and foibles and live with the judgement you render upon yourself. I think I am probably doing okay, to all intents and purposes. I have some properties, but I have no money to develop them. I am not accumulating debt, but I can't buy shiny things. I have the financial resources of a guppy, but I can swim along for long periods with little more than fresh water, a sprinkle of food, and a gulp of air. I am a good person, and gosh darn it people like me.

So it seemed like there was but one road open before me, and that road led to Europe. And in an effort to change my ways (although at great personal cost to myself and those around me), I set off to do that.

And right this second I am sitting in Europe, typing this book (on a typewriter! Can you believe that?), having my Hemingway moment like I always thought I would, working on closing the loop of this long unfinished education of mine, aiming at a new profession (art dealer or something?), and undertaking a kind of reverse Christopher Columbus voyage of discovery, but to the Old World.

How can that be bad? Yes, I could have been something

else by now, but I am also learning that I can only be who and what I am at any given moment, based on what I have managed to accomplish so far in life, and right now I am a 48-year-old exchange student in Europe.

Willkommen in Deutschland

Quite unlike it would have for a young English nobleman or member of the landed gentry in, say, 1600 or so, my Grand Tour – my finishing year in Europe – would not start with a ride with my teacher or tour guide in a private carriage from London to the coast of England, followed by a leisurely or angst-ridden sailing (a lot depended on the weather and general level of drunkenness of the crew) of the English Channel to Ostende, Belgium, or Calais, France, whereupon one would continue once again by private coach or make one's way by boat toward the heart of Europe.

No, my tour of Europe would start with a solitary bus ride from my former island home in British Columbia, Canada, to the ferry that would carry me to the mainland of the province and the large city of Vancouver, and then another bus ride and a commuter train trip to the airport, which would be the jumping-off point for the nine- or 10-hour flight to Europe.

This is a long and boring way to get from Point A to Point Airport. It is uncomfortable and inconvenient. Why do I often have to do things this way? Well, it is inexpensive, that cannot be argued. Having someone take me is a great expense to them, at least in terms of time, but mainly, I end up going alone because I have no ties left when I am ready to leave one phase of life and move on to the next one. Even if people weren't already so busy, there are seldom any left who would care to move my person from where it is to the airport.

The journey didn't start that well for other reasons, too. I was already exhausted on the way to the airport. I had worked all summer in an east-coast office of the federal government of Canada, in Prince Edward Island, in order to be close enough to my farm property there and do a little organizing and building on the land. I also wanted to get reacquainted with some of my stuff.

Years ago, when I stopped living in Montreal, I had moved almost everything I had at the time to PEI and stuffed it into three little buildings I had purchased and placed on the farm. I had always planned to move down there and stay, but it had never happened, and I rarely had the time or money to even get to the property after that, let alone develop it. But the ending of my ties in Victoria meant that I was free to work on this goal, even if in a limited way, and for four months I had worked weekdays in the office and on weekends on the farm to single-handedly put in the foundation of a future house. I worked every weekend except one (I just had to take one off) and then went back to British Columbia to move everything out of my girlfriend's basement (she kindly let me store things there until I could make it back) before heading off to Europe. She even had my youngest kid with her for some time that summer, until his mom came back to town and took him in.

Back in British Columbia, I insanely moved myself, helped my ex-girlfriend build a fence we always said we would build, and helped my previous ex-girlfriend move house. That previous ex-girlfriend let me stay with her for the few days it took to accomplish all of this, and that really helped, as I was otherwise homeless in the city. Near Victoria, I only have a small building lot with an unfinished cabin on it that I call the 'man cave,' and it was stuffed with the rest of my belongings.

When I finally headed to the airport, the heavy lifting was done, and I was completely used up. Don't panic, but a third ex-girlfriend offered to see me off at the airport. Before you go all crazy on me, you should know that I had very few girlfriends in my life, and that my relationships with them were, as I say elsewhere, getting shorter and shorter. Still, they were wonderful people who I obviously cared about, and I always tried to stay on their good sides. Some people don't, I know, but what is the point of that?

This one was an actress who I thought was resourceful, resilient, edgy, and realistic all at the same time, and I was able to spend my last hour in Canada with her after not seeing her for quite a long time.

We had met in worse places than an airport, and we thought the whole thing was quite funny. We spent the time finding a lost Australian passport and turning it in to the authorities, eating awful Asian take-out food, and then getting secretly engaged with an eternity ring I happened to have with me (I didn't want to leave all my valuables behind).

This was not done on the off chance that we would both put our lives in a certain kind of order and live happily ever after. It was more like throwing out some kind of anchor to the place I came from, to the memory of my past life and how it might have looked if we were both simply different from what we really are.

It was also then completely impossible but not unserious, so that today I have to remind her that it was a *secret* engagement, not a *mock* one. She seems to forget that regularly. She even spoke about it on a television show, saying she was sure I had even written her out of this book.

My flight eventually took off, and it amounted to being strapped into a huge, flying cigar tube from a discount cigar, like human sardines, all with their assorted national viruses in tow, from which I would soon catch a cold, as I always do after an international flight. And the whole while, I was not hurtling toward the art centre of the world, but rather toward the cold, metal, industrial heart of Germany.

Mannheim: that is where I would be studying for the next year. Even though it is not the arts epicentre that Paris, London, or Florence are, it is still in Europe, and thanks to the city's very central location on the Continent, it is close enough to all of those centres to make visiting them quite easy.

Although I had never been to Mannheim, touching down in Frankfurt and being back in Europe felt a little bit like going back in time or going home. Just a decade or so before (not nearly so far back as to rejoin those English nobles we left hanging back there a bit earlier) I had last been here. Eleven years ago. I had a hard time believing that it had been so long. I had come here so often before, and I had always loved Europe. How had I let 11 years go by without once again setting foot in the place?

For a dedicated Europhile like myself, this is a bad state of affairs, like a gap in your resume (or your front teeth, when you are not Vanessa Paradis). This is how you can tell you have been on the wrong path in life, as of late. Eleven years, at this stage, is almost a quarter of my life. What exactly had I been doing during all that time that was more important to me than being here? Sure, I had gotten divorced from my German wife and suddenly had much less reason to come and visit here. And sure, I probably did lots of other useful, important, or interesting things in the intervening years. But I tell you, Europe was always on my mind, yet somehow I managed to avoid the place. I went on other holidays to other spots. I moved around Canada. I lived in Los Angeles. But landing here again was quite an experience in which I suddenly realized how strange it is to see that you have simply been letting yourself down, letting your own dreams pass, and that nothing and nobody was ever truly standing in your way. Nobody was stopping you but yourself. Nobody kept you from packing a bag and investing the nine or so hours it takes to get here. Nobody.

Oh well. The first thing I noticed upon touch down was that Germany had not changed much since the last time I had been here. But I also felt immediately that, no matter how much had physically changed or stayed the same here during all that time, I had changed and that I would be seeing Europe again for the first time, through fresh eyes. This time I was here to study art and not to be a photographer or tourist, and somehow, this was going to help. On all of my previous trips as a photographer, trying to focus in on the classic European sights and stereotypical notion of European beauty, I had always had a niggling suspicion that the place, for all our connotations of it, is not just one big, pretty film set. Not every square inch of it is attractive. You have to be really quite selective about where you point a camera so that you don't bring home a whole lot of pictures of things that would make friends seeing them cross the place off their must-see or bucket list. If you hail from the prairies, like I do, from a rusting Midlands town, or from the Outback of Australia, you already know what I am talking about. There is plenty of beauty here, there, and everywhere, but sometimes you have to be selective about finding it. It is distributed in a haphazardly erratic fashion and in a maddeningly small ratio. Yes, beauty is also in the eye of the beholder, but sometimes it is obscured by factories and power lines.

Surely some of our fine, young English noblemen from earlier had to traverse some rather desolate areas of forlorn scrubland or otherwise unenticing terrain before they saw their first towering cathedral or sunrise (or sunset, if not much of a morning person) over the canals of Venice. My trip would be no different. Europe, no matter how much I want it to be, is no fairy tale setting, and this time, I was ready for that. This time I would be studying art, and thanks to museums and galleries, all of the beautiful things would be conveniently bundled together and accessible to me for the price of admission. As a photographer, they had been all over the place, or obscured by graffiti.

Art.

Art is beauty. Art is the science of finding pleasing form and design in all things, if possible, and handily leaving out

Bentley Bryce Finley

the soulless, empty spaces in between. So, on this trip, in this finishing year, I would not have to (much) confront the ugly but ever-present underbelly of the place, trying to make aesthetic sense out of it with a camera, but rather could spend my time seeking out its best corners, seeing them from their best angles, and drinking in the storied, cultured layers of beauty and refinement captured and housed in the great museums and galleries. I would breath in the light and regard the air with a fresh gaze and feel the return stares of a thousand portraits and imagine that I could feel what sorrows and joys a thousand sculptors and painters had felt during the making of their art and what thoughts were running through the minds of the sitters or other participants. But first I had to get from the airport in Frankfurt to my new home in Mannheim, which required a short stretch of train travel through an area of Germany pretty well slavishly devoted to that underbelly.

Every country has its good and bad sides. Some angles are better than others. And Europe (I realize it is not a country), the place of so many of my dreams, can never, ever, possibly live up to the shrine of conceptions I have built to it in my head over all these years. Germany is a prime example of this. It simply cannot possibly match, in real life, the advertising campaigns it has somehow placed in my mind. Too many people here (and by that, I mean especially now that I am in Mannheim) do not know how to use a litter barrel, for instance, or say hello when they pass you on the sidewalk, or speak German, for that matter. Those are just a few examples of the unrecognizable, faceless masses of people I encounter every day who are letting my dream down. No, my dreams of Europe will forever remain trapped in the former age that gave them birth, an age that never really existed or that I was born too late to witness, the age of films like *Chitty Chitty Bang Bang*, *The Sound of Music*, or, at the very outside, *Cabaret*.

The almost completely forgotten Canadian children's

38

television show *George*, about a troublesome St. Bernard dog that gets shipped back home to Switzerland and lives with an ex-pat American pilot and his family, is almost single-handedly responsible for fueling my desire to go overseas and is unduly responsible for my being so in love with the place. But as I said a while back, until they actually install wastebaskets on people's backs here, it will never again live up to my ideal, squeaky-clean image of the place, where everywhere you look is worthy of turning into a postcard.

Still, this time around at least, I did not have a poor introduction. The flight over was great. My extremely discounted air carrier had been excellent. Everything had gone off without a hitch. The whole trip reminded me to never read the nasty reviews left online by disgruntled travellers on websites with names like AirlineHell.com or Uhhuh,andwherearemybags.org. I had read some of them before leaving which would have made anyone think that my discount flight would surely end in a ball of flames or a mushroom cloud, whereas the flight only pushed back from the gate a bit late. What did I care? I was going away for a whole year! What matter is a little bit of time when you are staring at a dream you have been thinking about, if off and on, for your entire life? Soon I would be standing regularly in front of 600-year-old paintings or in the naves of 1000-year-old churches. Soon, time would take on a whole new meaning for me, and I would become part of a continuum that I had never much considered before.

Still, there is no escaping reality completely, and there were still things to do before I would be in any art galleries or museums. Arrival in Frankfurt on a discount airline means a bus trip from the tarmac to the air terminal and then an interesting walk through a building, the length of which will never be measured by mortal man. Customs is easy, a matter of personal choice of taking either the 'something to declare' lane or the 'I have no drugs on me' one, both of which seem to have nobody patrolling them. The train station, the next necessary component for reaching Mannheim, is conveniently glued onto the side of the air terminal. No taxis are required here, which saves money in a country where transportation is not exactly cheap.

Perhaps this one item is the one I most have still in common with that unknown English nobleman of the 17th century making a similar trip. Travel expenses can be enormous. Nowadays, one pays the rather exorbitant price of 23 Euros to travel the mere 72 kilometres or so from Frankfurt to Mannheim on the train. At home in Canada, I can take a local bus for 25 kilometres, from downtown Victoria to our airport or our ferry terminal, for a grand total of about $2.25, about one and a half Euros at this moment. If I go to the ferry instead of the airport, I can take the bus on the other side of the water another 35 kilometres to the bigger Vancouver airport for a similar price. I had been living in the land of cheap transportation, and I didn't even know it.

But that is what travel does: it opens your eyes to things you had not seen, even if those things are at home.

German personal service also still leaves a little to be desired, just as it always has. I am sorry to report it, but that has not changed one bit on any of my trips to the place. My first taste of it this time around was on that train trip to Mannheim. The conductor, who was dressed a lot like a waiter in a light blue shirt and dark blue vest, entered my otherwise deserted cabin and said something that, to my unpracticed German ear, sounded a lot like, "Wollen Sie etwas bestellen?", which would mean, "Would you like to order anything?" I answered, "Nein" and went back to gazing out the window at the graffiti-covered fences zipping by. I was quite absorbed in watching this passing underbelly when I noticed the man still standing in the doorway, fairly gaping at my answer. I turned back toward him and asked if that is what he had said. He heartily denied that he had but also neglected to tell me what he had, in fact, said. This was kind of a stand-off, wasn't it? A little while passed and he asked to see my ticket. Now I realized he was not the waiter but the conductor, and he cleared away any remaining doubt I might still have been harbouring by repeating his original question in exactly the same words, this time inexplicably completely understandable to my untuned ear: "Sind Sie neu eingestiegen?" or "Did you just board?"

I decided to play along with his little game of not answering directly and said, "Ah, but you are dressed exactly like the waiter." This met with another blank stare, but I handed him my ticket anyway, and he gave it a snort, handed it back, and stormed off down the corridor. The lessons here are many: if you are the conductor of a train and not the waiter, wear the proper conductor's uniform of a hat and jacket, along with the light shirt and dark vest. And if you are a visitor who has not been to Europe for many years, don't automatically assume that a conductor's uniform even still includes a jacket and a cap or that there even are waiters on trains anymore. Times change.

My meeting party at the central railway station in Mannheim was late arriving to pick me up, and because I was so early, I had twice as much time on my hands as planned. Although the city was right in front of me and the entrance to the station, I did not feel ready to go exploring it with my luggage in tow and my energy level at zero. I decided to spend the hour or two I had simply crouched outside the train station, propped up against a post, people watching. That lasted only a moment, as a local paranoid-schizophrenic immediately made his way over and latched onto me and talked to me pretty much the entire time. He told me about whatever fell into his poor, addled head in a swirling stream of passing thoughts. If you know anything about the average paranoid-schizophrenic, you know that you can't lead the conversation anywhere, unless you are equally chomping at the bit to discuss various people likely to be following you, who killed J.F.K, or the (I guess) un-secret inner workings of the C.I.A., or preferably all three at the same time. So we talked about these things and pretty much the whole ball of Masonic-military-industrial-complex-terrorist wax.

It is unfortunate that I study art and do not know more about the inner workings of the seven families who control the world economy, or the intricacies of the street layout of Barack Obama's hometown (in Kenya). I should also note that nearly this entire conversation was held in English. Paranoid-schizophrenics, if they were autistic instead, would be the extremely high-functioning ones. This would also be one of the few times that any German would voluntarily speak with me, in any language, for approximately the first five months of my stay.

Another student from my new school eventually arrived to deliver me to my new student accommodation, a near-empty, monk-like cell in one of those awful 1970s modernist buildings that are so far removed from what the ideal Europe I talked about is supposed to look like.

These things were built to replace huge swatches of the city that were bombed in World War II and are absolutely everywhere and now constitute one of the longest-lasting travesties of that war and form nearly the only remaining scar upon the land. Whereas the battlefields have been grown over by nature or reclaimed by farmers, the rows upon rows of post-war buildings continue to blight an urban landscape that well might never be rehabilitated without future catastrophes.

As much as I love modern architecture and its proponents like Gropius and Le Corbusier, someone among their ilk has got a lot of explaining to do. Some number of nameless practitioners of the style after the war spread the language a little too far and a little too thin. And how did Germany, a country with such a strong vernacular architecture and so many diverse and interesting regional building styles ever go so far down the path of a one-size-fits-all modernism that reached almost every corner of the country? Large swaths of the country look like high-rise versions of suburban America, if nondescript ranchers or bungalows could be uprooted and stacked atop one another.

How did Germany turn its back on everything it had built in the last 600 to 1000 years and go in for this stuff? The only thing that could go further in wrecking my ideal image of an ideal Germany would be if Black Forest cuckoo clock makers abandoned the woodsy cabins and chalets of their creations and turned out square, lifeless, modernist cuckoo clocks. As it is, these clock makers are nearly the only arbiters of traditional German architecture left, and their creations are so small that nobody could ever live in them. (Okay, I have to say, I have seen such modernist cuckoo clocks already, so whatever. I was just trying to make a point.)

As fate would have it, just such a cubic, modernist mess was to be my home for the coming year. It had no charm. I was not enthralled by this. The room itself had very little going for it. A single bed that was more of a sofa than anything else, a bare linoleum floor (actually much easier to keep clean when you have no broom, vacuum cleaner, or detergents), a shelf, a table and chair, and a sink and mirror. The bathroom and shower are down the hall. The kitchen, right outside my door, is a bit of a problem. It appears that, just like on the streets outside, the local residents don't know how to deal with garbage and are a little bit challenged overall in the cleanliness department. From the looks of it, at least one or two of the city's worst offenders lived right here on my floor of 10 apartments and one kitchen. This will have to be addressed over time.

My introduction to Mannheim was thus not entirely underwhelming or overwhelming. This room, despite its unwelcoming attitude, was now my home, and keeping that floor clean would be a cinch.

It is at moments like these that we make important but

microscopic decisions about how we are going to live the rest of our lives. These moments go on to add to and blend with all of our other experiences and form our outlook on life. I am known in most circles as a 'glass-half-empty' kind of guy, even when the glass in question is clearly half full. Yet the most fantastic things have happened to me in this life. And they keep happening to me. I have worked in the most interesting things. I have had the most rewarding relationships with the most beautiful women (you think I kid, but I do not). One of them gave me two of the greatest kids. The point is that, however we choose to react to any given situation goes on to colour our lives from that moment on.

Normally, in such a situation, I would have let myself go on to experience a moment or two (anywhere from half a day to a few weeks) of regret and sadness at my current situation, a certain sinking feeling at the turn my life had taken. But not this time. This time I was in Europe, and I still refused to think anything bad of the place – yet.

So I simply chose not to go to that dark place in my psyche, and I immediately felt better for it. Look at what the European experience was doing for me already! A half day in the country (I know, Europe is not a country) and here I was already looking at things in a more positive light.

Handy proverbs sprang to mind. The old adage that "it can't get any worse" came immediately to mind and seemed completely applicable here. My former girlfriend, Su, had said we have to choose happiness and that it is hard work. Maybe all her lessons on the subject had not been delivered in vain. So in that moment, I chose happiness. I also chose not to press my luck by hanging about such morbid, drab surroundings one minute longer than necessary and immediately set off to scout out the neighbourhood and round up something to eat for dinner.

Both of those endeavours (checking out the neighbourhood and finding food) turned out to be further exercises in making good life choices at forks in the mental road where one could consciously choose something other than happiness. The immediate neighbourhood around my new lodgings must have been a favourite of wartime Allies or been vacant back then because all of the buildings in the area were of the nondescript, post-war modern type, except for one huge brick building across the street.

That one building seemed a bit out of place, older and more traditional than the rest. It was also much bigger than a building needs to be, it occurred to me. It was really more of a complex, and it was the only building in the neighbourhood that displayed any style at all. It was really quite nice. Later investigation would reveal it to be the local prison.

My less-than-stellar introduction to my new life in Germany continued as I walked farther and farther from my new home and failed to uncover any kind of shop. When I finally did run across some, they were firmly closed. By checking a few signs in stores, I realized that it was not only too late in the day to be shopping, it was the wrong day altogether to be looking for open businesses. It was Sunday, and I suddenly realized that nearly everything is closed here on Sundays. I finally came across a service station that had a little store open, and from amongst all the junk food, I decided to buy peanuts and beer to make up my first meal in Germany and walked home to my barren cell, at least no longer starving.

In the morning, my new life in Europe began in earnest. My university had asked me to be in Germany by that particular date, to attend a kind of kick-off for the upcoming school year. As I was in my final year but with less than a full year's worth of courses left to take, I would be able to study at about half the usual course load and work the other half of the time in the school's International Office, helping my fellow exchange students get through their daily lives.

After my initial visit to the school, it became clear that

my light course load would leave me with tons of free time, not the least of which would be the 10 or 11 days before any of my courses would actually start. Although I was freshly landed in Europe and newly embarked upon living out one of my longest held dreams, I couldn't help thinking about how I could have better used this windfall of spare time back in Canada, finishing up loose ends and avoiding the rushing around I had endured right at the end. Every rose has its thorn, I guess. Or every half-filled glass has its other half – the half-empty void above it – pressing down on it.

The university campus is about five kilometres from downtown, so it takes a walk, two streetcars, and another walk to get there (unless one has a car or a bicycle), but the journey and the setting are both beautiful. The streetcar that finally deposits you just outside one of our buildings takes the five-kilometre trek along the south side of the quite beautiful Neckar River, and the campus itself is sparklingly modern (not like the dingy, much older modern buildings that make up the rest of the city). And it all sits on the edge of a cornfield or sugar beet plot (depending on the season) that touches the outskirts of town at this place.

Altogether it is a very pleasant place to spend part of each day, but only a few of my German language classes will take place here. The rest of my studies (the art history classes) will involve museum and gallery visits. There will be virtually no class time in those courses, so I can quickly immerse myself in the art that is hanging around, and that will mean starting right here in Mannheim and then working my way methodically outward in ever-widening circles. That will include the nearby cities of Heidelberg, Worms, Speyer, Mainz, Frankfurt, Stuttgart, and many others.

It sounds like a plan I should get started on.

A Small Town in Germany

My town – my city – in Germany is not a tourist attraction in anyone's books, not even for Germans. Mannheim does not appear on any 'must see' list of cities to visit before or even shortly after you die. No tourist would take time out of the busy itinerary of an otherwise exciting world tour to make a pity stop here. This semi-industrial city on the Rhine, even if a traveller were touring great portions of the river by water or road, would not likely be a planned destination, and the visitor could easily regret it if it were.

The American writer, Mark Twain, clearly enamoured of our nearby neighbour Heidelberg when he visited our area and wrote about it in his more than 100-year-old travel book, *A Tramp Abroad*, only pops into Mannheim on a few occasions and mostly regrets it. One such case: "One day we took the train and went down to Mannheim to see *King Lear* played in German. It was a mistake. We sat in our seats three whole hours and never understood anything but the thunder and lightning; and even that was reversed to suit German ideas, for the thunder came first and the lightning followed after."

To be fair, Twain doesn't mention much about Mannheim outside of visits to the theatre. Maybe his visits were mostly disturbing because of the playhouse: "Another time, we went to Mannheim and attended a shivaree – otherwise an opera – the one called *Lohengrin*. The banging and slamming and booming and crashing were something beyond belief. The racking and pitiless pain of it remains stored up in my memory alongside the memory of the time that I had my teeth fixed."

Well, to be absolutely fair again, that doesn't have a lot

to do with Mannheim at street-level, and a lot of people don't like Wagner operas anyway. But overall, the impression given by these 100-year-old experiences still seems to hold true in my city today.

Although we have a large train station that is always packed with people, few of them appear to be tourists of any kind. Most foreigners seem to be exchange students, like me, and they can't always choose where they will end up. And although we are situated on both the Rhine and Neckar rivers, passing tour boats seldom stop at one of our docks. One can almost imagine them gliding past under the cover of darkness as a way to avoid allegations of constant snubbing. But then, Mannheim twinkles while passengers snooze, wrapped snuggly in their bunks, and miss any chance they might have of changing their opinions of the place.

Mannheim surely must have some visitors who at least drop in for a quick look, but I am not sure why. There really isn't much to see under its gritty and industrial, rebuilt-after-bombing, modern-architecture-eyesore cloak. It has not always been that way, mind you. Mannheim was home to much beauty and art at one time, and since it will be my home for the coming year, I will eventually spend a lot of time following such threads back to their origins to discover some of that, both what was once here and what remains. Mannheim will serve as the starting and finishing point of all my European discoveries as well. Rather than being a series of Point A to Point B adventures, my travels here will radiate out constantly from and always return to Mannheim. Because of work and school, I can't just take off. It could be worse: I could not be here at all. That is what happened to Mozart, as we will soon see.

They say that when you come to Mannheim, you cry twice: once when you arrive and once when you leave. To that end, the town fathers conveniently supply foreign students with a Welcome Box that just happens to contain two packets of tissues, among other goodies. I used up both packets right off the bat, not because it was so bad here, but rather due to the killer cold I had picked up in the airplane on the way overseas. My fellow students and I, and everyone who had travelled with us on our planes, had of course brought every virus known to man to our new home, and these were now mixing and mingling and having wild parties in our heads. Crying later, if it happened at all, was going to require more tissues.

Mannheim is an extremely good example of an international melting pot city, even outside of flu season. There are dozens of nationalities represented here, but the one you will notice most is the Turkish branch. Mannheim is, in a way, the new Turkey, and the old Turkey has, in a way, moved to Mannheim.

Since Germany first invited Turkish workers here in the 1960s, Mannheim has been socking them in. For guest workers at least, Mannheim has always been a desirable destination: half the people they knew already lived here. Although other nationalities are present in the city statistics, Turkish people still represent 30 to 60% of the population, depending on which Stadtteil (borough or neighbourhood) you are talking about.

All I can say is that there are simply an incredible number of Turkish people roaming the streets here, and at all hours of the day and night, even when the German-German portion of the population is sleeping or otherwise holed up (on days off or when all the businesses are closed on Sundays). Not so the Turkish Mannheimers. When the Germans are asleep, Turkish restaurants are wide awake, and the Dönerladen (the shops that sell the ubiquitous rolled-up Turkish sandwich) are in full swing, with line-ups stretching down the block. If it has to do with food and Turkish people, it will particularly be crowded when the rest of the country is snoring.

Entire families – and from the look of it, mostly extended families, four or more generations deep – are underway past midnight in search of food and conversation. These packs will either be just heading out around the time most people are rolling down their shutters, or they will be just heading back from such an outing when the town church bells strike the first hours of the morning. Lively little children will be running around under the lamplight with their families slowly drifting down the sidewalks behind them, an hour or so after carriages turn into pumpkins and other kids have been in bed half the night.

Anyhow, this makes Mannheim a strangely, highly Turkish experience at times. Our mosque is the largest in Germany. Döner, or Döner kebab, is by far the best fast food in the world and can be purchased approximately every 10 feet or so on some streets. I never had really heard of it until I came to Mannheim.

If Mannheim is not the biggest at something, then it is the second or third biggest usually. Besides that mosque, we have either the second or third largest train station, population, or otherwise, in our state. We have the second-largest John Deere installation in the world, outside of home-base operations in the United States. Mannheim is the second-last place chemical giant BASF called home before it moved across the river to Ludwigshafen. It depends on what you read or who you talk to, but a few things are certain: we are located in the warmest region of the country, and even Wolfgang Amadeus Mozart wanted to stay here and eventually married a former Mannheim girl.

At the beginning, when I first arrived here, all of these little facts and characteristics seemed like a confusing mix. For instance, all of this local Turkishness means there is sometimes very little integration of the largest masses here. Mannheim is a very diverse city but one with a clear and enduring cultural gulf. For our purposes, as students here, it makes for very little language exchange sometimes, unless you are also studying Turkish, a great idea for this location.

The clash of the old and the new, even as it extends to the buildings around town, seems unresolvable. I have to formally register my shock and awe that, while my university is housed in some very nice, modern buildings, it is *not* the university that is located in the attractive baroque Schloss (castle) in the centre of the city. Sure, my university is the state university, housed in an attractive, ultra-modern, cube-like structure surrounding a strangely deserted, mostly locked courtyard, located about 5 km from downtown, right on the outskirts of town and possessing a name that, in English, makes it sound more like a high school than a university. But the city university, located in the castle in the heart of the old city, is the one everybody knows. It kind of defeats the purpose of going overseas to study in some ancient and hallowed institution if it is not the one the town is known for.

Someone obviously thought Mannheim was a decent place to plunk down a small city, at the confluence of two important and navigable rivers. They say the name Mannheim (Mann*en*heim at the start) was first recorded in 766 in a legal document that still exists. The name means 'Manno's place' where Manno would be the nickname or short form for any kind of slightly longer German moniker such as Hermann or Hartmann. So some Hermann or Hartmann or something similar was the original inhabitant, most likely.

Historically, the city graduated from being a village in 1606, when Frederick IV, Elector Palatine, commenced construction of a fortress and an Innenstadt (city centre), oddly, for the time, laid out in a circular grid where only the blocks have numbers and the streets have no names.

The city got flattened a number of times, always in fighting with neighbours, and especially in the Thirty Years War (circa 1622 or so) and during the thankfully shorter but no more pleasing Nine Years War (circa 1689). With a new elector (Karl III Philip), the capital of the Electorate of the Palatinate moved from nearby Heidelberg to

Mannheim, and things really got rolling in the square city. The place got that new palace that now houses the university (also flattened during World War II but reconstructed afterward). That palace, started in 1720, was meant to be the largest in Europe and a prime specimen of baroque style and with it, Enlightened Absolutism.

It took 40 years to complete and – in keeping with the 'Mannheim is either first, second, or third' thing – eventually featured one more window than the competing palace at Versailles. The thing had 500 rooms! Versailles was still bigger, but the Mannheim rulers had that one extra window. This was important because, through some complicated reasoning of the day, properties were valued or taxed by the number of windows they had (glass was expensive), and in that way somehow showed the financial resources of their owners. Although Versailles was in a different country and subject to different taxes, somehow the accomplishment of installing that last window made Mannheim the mental or moral winner in a contest of wills to display wealth and power that nobody probably knew was even taking place.

All of this show-off Absolutism came at a price, however. The palace construction cost nearly 10 times the predicted budget and threw the ruling family into a kind of gilded poverty (much, much more enjoyable than your or my poverty could ever be, now or then) wherein, sadly, many of the rooms of the new palace could not be decorated or furnished for lack of funds. It took generations to pay off the debt.

Despite wars and the occasional levelling of the city, Mannheim – back in the day – was called a sight to see by some. In 1819, British Royal Navy officer Norwich Duff, on a Grand Tour of the continent, saw a different Mannheim than we know today. Ironically, before all of the supposed awareness we enjoy today concerning universal education, hidden sewers, environmentalism, or picking up your trash, Duff saw a Mannheim where "the streets are broad and at right angles to each other" [okay, they still are], "and is one of the most airy clean towns I have seen in Germany."

Really? Duff might be saddened to know that Mannheim eventually went a very different way on that. Most of our descent into dirty has to do with pollution: the light, personal kind where a litter barrel would be a great help, and the heavy industrial kind from manufacturing and chemical companies. A local boy, Karl Drais, did once try to save the planet by inventing the bicycle here, but, in two offsetting moves, Friedrich Engelhorn also founded BASF nearby, now likely the world's largest chemical company, and Karl Benz patented the first motor car here in 1886, which kind of cancelled out any environmental benefits the bicycle might have had.

Our area has an almost inbred preference for the industrial. Drais's bicycle, although quite useful at the time of its invention (a famine had killed off many local horses, then used for transportation), was temporarily outlawed when it was found that far too many of them were beginning to clog the streets and footpaths of the region.

All of this industrial activity had its cost. BASF, although started more than 100 years ago now, made that move across the river and into the neighbouring state of Rheinland-Pfalz when Mannheim feared the pollution and proposed higher taxes to deal with it than did our neighbours to the west. BASF, as a sign of thanks, expanded into its own industrial city to something bordering on 14 km long and 4 km wide and happily pays its taxes on all of that to our neighbours on the other side of the river, instead. Whatever pollution they do put out goes into the air and water we more or less share, depending on which way the wind is blowing.

Two locals (Karl Lanz and Johann Schütte) built airships in Mannheim to compete with the more famous Zeppelin works from southern Germany at about the time Germany was ramping up for their first go at world war.

This helped establish Mannheim as a prime military target, leading the city to become the first civilian settlement ever to be bombed from the air in an international conflict.

After the city built up quite a collection of manufacturing and chemical plants, Germany's enemies saw fit to follow it up with much more widespread bombings during World War II. These not only targeted those local manufacturing capabilities, they also almost completely razed the city in what some call the first deliberate terror bombing of civilians.

But life in Mannheim, looked at through the perspective of many centuries, was not all bad. The city was nice enough to visit, and it attracted its share of cultural and artistic luminaries. Wolfgang Amadeus Mozart started coming to the city as a child performer when his father figured out how to make a buck off the kid. The first time was around 1762-63, and you can just imagine the state of child labour laws then. But no matter. The work was well paid, much better than what other kids had to do at the time to earn their keep. Still, even fairly comfortable middle-class (there was no real middle-class then) families like the Mozarts were in need of earning a little money off the sweat of a child's brow.

Later, when Mozart was working as a disgruntled and by then underpaid (the child star aura always wears off) court musician in his native Salzburg, Austria, he headed out on a job-seeking tour of the various royal courts of Europe, hoping to land a better arrangement. In Mannheim, he met and worked with members of the prestigious local orchestra – the best in Europe at the time – and fell in love with the daughter of one of the musicians. The daughter was Aloysia Weber, but on that trip (in 1777), Mozart failed to get a position in Mannheim at the big palace that was paying for all its windows and so continued on his way. With no offers in sight except back home in Salzburg (a place he dreaded returning to, even with an offer of four times his previous salary), he dropped back in on Mannheim for a final try and found not only no job but three other pieces of news: that the Webers had moved to Vienna, Aloysia was now a successful opera singer in Munich, and she was no longer interested in him. Mozart had not gotten the memo.

Mozart returned to Salzburg, then moved to Vienna to hang out his shingle as a freelance composer (it is strange to think that you could have once bought a song from W.A.M. in Mannheim, if not in Vienna). Mannheim's Weber family was still living in Vienna at that time, but in reduced circumstances, due to the father's death. Mozart took it upon himself to help out by moving in with them as a sort of lodger.

That led directly to Mozart's becoming interested in a second Weber girl, this time third daughter Constanze. They married and eventually had six children, only two of whom survived into adulthood.

Here both Mozart and his Mannheim story come to an end. Neither of his sons married or had children. Succeeding waves of destruction in Mannheim have removed most signs of his legacy here. A few plaques mark the places he stayed (the C&A department store is built near the location of a hotel he once stayed in), and the large church across from the palace, where he played the organ on Sundays, survives and is beautiful after the rebuilding of its bombed out shell.

It is sad and ironic that the local royal family would not or could not (all of those windows had exacted a very heavy price, indeed) employ Mozart and keep him engaged in Mannheim. All of the family's efforts at refinement pale in comparison to what would have been realized had Mozart stayed in Mannheim. Their efforts really did amount to, in the end, just window dressing.

Friedrich Schiller, the German writer and Goethe friend, spent some time in Mannheim as well. He had written his first (and probably most famous) play, *The*

Robbers, while attending military school and studying medicine in another city.

Later, when he was stationed as a regimental doctor in Stuttgart, he left his post there without permission to attend the first public performance of his play in Mannheim and received 14 days in jail for the breach. His ruler, Karl Eugen, Duke of Württemberg, also forbid him to publish any more such literary writings. That meant Schiller had to escape Stuttgart altogether, so he again passed through Mannheim heading north to Weimar. Goethe then got him back into writing literature instead of scientific papers, and the rest is history that has nothing to do with Mannheim, but the great man did live here from July, 1783, until April, 1785, and he did enjoy his first successes as a playwright here, though his one-year contract with the National Theatre was not renewed. So we will always have that. Schiller was also sick with malaria while here (something I have so far avoided) and he eventually headed off for greener pastures in Leipzig, getting Mannheim back by thus ducking financial difficulties that had crept up on him during his stay here.

We could go on about others: Goethe, Lessing (a great figure of the Enlightenment who once proposed to the daughter of Mannheim book dealer – and later, publisher – Christian Schwan), and others. But if Mannheim was ever home to them, it was always a second home or a temporary one. These great figures all went on to make some other place more famous. Even today, that curse remains. Mannheim proudly proclaims its fate of being the second largest city in the state, of having the second busiest train station – because that is the way it is. The city isn't nearly as visited as is nearby Heidelberg. People don't consider it to be as pretty as that city. One of Mannheim's twin cities is the ever-so-appropriate Windsor, Ontario, Canada. I, being Canadian, know that you could not make this stuff up if you tried: the pairing is too keen. If you have never seen the cold, industrial exterior of Windsor, the original town without pity, located just across a bridge from Detroit, a city now emptying itself out, you could just come to Mannheim instead. Plus, you would only be three hours away from Paris by train, something you cannot claim in Windsor.

So my art history tour of Europe and my year in which to do it would both start in Mannheim. Luckily, the city does have some art treasures to keep the art lover going for a while. I would start at the Kunsthalle Mannheim, pretty much the city's art gallery. It lies just outside the Quadrat centre of town (where the streets have no names, you might recall), so it actually possesses a street address (Moltkestrasse 9) and is only about five city blocks away from the main entrance of that second-biggest train station and then a hard right at the picturesque city water tower.

The Kunsthalle specializes, probably due to its youthful age (founded 1907), in art of the 19th and 20th centuries but also features some graphic work from the 15th to end of the 18th centuries. It also has an archive for children's art, which has a special connection to a former Kunsthalle director and his family.

When I first visited, the gallery was drastically reduced in size due to an ongoing renovation and planned addition of a new building. The new building has been needed ever since the original was erected in 1907. That one, although a quite beautiful example of the Jugendstil (or Art Nouveau) style, was put up in haste as a temporary building to house an international art and garden show (garden design was once a very important component of the visual or architectural arts). It was meant to be disassembled after the show, but when it was emptied, the town fathers thought twice about demolishing it and decided to install the city painting collection there instead.

That collection started out being so small that it was not enough to fill even the ground floor of the recently vacated building. It never would fill it unless the city entered upon a path of being an art collector of sorts, something the city fathers were not looking forward to. The gallery director at the time had a sly solution to this: he mounted a show of the best modern French and German art of the day and made sure to post the current asking prices next to most of the 100 or so pieces he had borrowed from leading art dealers and gallerists.

This gave both the city government and every visitor to the exhibition of modern masterpieces a pretty clear idea of exactly what it was going to take to give Mannheim an admirable art collection. Even the art gallery board thought their director's choices were a bit too cutting edge, too expensive, and, especially, too French. They felt the pieces on display were too much aimed at knowledgeable art lovers and not easy enough (they meant beautiful enough) for average citizens to appreciate.

The director countered that if the gallery collected according to the tastes of the day (and those of the viewing public), it would end up with a collection of little value, and he was right. In a kind of compromise, the Kunsthalle went on to acquire a little bit of both: quite a number of paintings from expensive, leading German artists of the time who nobody remembers today, and a whole bunch of much more affordable and less appreciated works of that time that are now remarkably loved and incredibly valuable (from Manet, Monet, Pissarro, Corot, Van Gogh, and others, for example).

Under a later director (G. F. Hartlaub), the gallery began amassing 20th century works, also unloved at the time but now highly prized, from the French Fauves to the German groups *Die Brucke* and *Blauer Reiter*. Hartlaub also coined the phrase (for a 1925 exhibition) 'Neue Sachlichkeit' (The New Objectivity), which was the art of German Expressionists during the Weimar Republic between the two world wars.

This kind of ultra-modern collecting soon got Hartlaub into hot water with those pesky National Socialists who were coming into power, and 86 paintings from the gallery (plus eight sculptures, 491 watercolours, and many other works) were seized by the Nazis as degenerate art, not fit for public consumption.

Most of those works simply disappeared, but some turned up at auction in 1939 in Switzerland (besides simply taking the works down so they wouldn't corrupt people's morals, the Nazis wanted to sell them in foreign countries to gather up hard cash for future war efforts). But they never came back to Mannheim. Of course, all this was within the rights of the government and the limits of the law of the time, so pieces by Chagall, Nolde, Delaunay, and many others ended up being sold to museums and collectors from Basel to New York but never needed to be repatriated back to the gallery that had first paid for them.

The gallery is still home to many great pieces, but none are earth shattering (those ones were lost in the seizure mentioned above), although many by the likes of Caspar David Friedrich, Alfred Sisley, Eugene Delacroix, Camille Pissarro, Paul Cezanne, Oskar Kokoschka, Erich Heckel, Karl Schmidt-Rottluff, Edvard Munch, and others are there to see.

The gallery's collection of drawings is also fascinating, with many interesting works by Henri de Toulouse-Lautrec, Edgar Degas, Paul Signac, Edvard Munch, Pablo Picasso, and more.

So little was on display on my first visit (things have since improved) that shortly after, I went back to my room and reverted to my old habit of studying pictures from books in order to see them. I had a copy of the Kunsthalle's handbook from 1983 among a batch of old art books I had purchased, and I flipped through it to see images of the works missing from the walls.

Because I had come all this way to study art up close and not in books, this setback in my new hometown was initially a bit of a stressor, due to this gallery renovation. I decided to add a new way to appreciate what I was not seeing up close by sketching the most interesting drawings and paintings in the book.

Copying artworks certainly forces you to closely consider what you are seeing. I leave it to the professional artists or art students to set up their easels in public galleries and to go about copying the masterpieces. I only sketch in private, to make myself really consider each part of the piece and not just gaze at it for a few seconds and move on. It works for me to get to know the pieces better, and I have been doing it since this first anticlimactic visit to the Kunsthalle in Mannheim near the start of my trip.

My amateur art certainly doesn't belong in a museum, but the Kunsthalle coincidentally has a place in its heart for such efforts. The son of former director G. F. Hartlaub (Felix, who disappeared in Berlin during military service in May, 1945) had a gigantic show of his childhood drawings on the day I visited the gallery.

These were amazing, detailed, scribbled imaginings on every subject of interest to a child. Felix went on to become somewhat famous after his death, when his many letters and even books were published. You might not know him, but this Felix Hartlaub is an interesting, true son of Mannheim, a thing quite in contrast to the more famous but transient and outside leading lights who only settled and created here for short periods of time (look him up someday if you get the chance).

Although there is much more than this to see in Mannheim, ironically – and like those other luminaries – I too would have to get out of town to truly expand my artistic horizons. That is what I would work on next.

And that would require a bicycle.

Roule, Roule

The bicycle was made for Europe, and Europe (probably unbeknownst to itself) was made for the bicycle. I have always known this. On my first trip here 31 years ago, right after graduating from high school, I brought with me a brand-new Raleigh touring bike with panniers. I wanted to use it on a European tour that never took place. I bought the bike, I did the practice rides, but that was it. The dream has always remained a dream.

Of course it has; I am reminded of it here constantly. Much of the terrain here is perfectly suited to two-wheeling, it being largely as flat as a pancake and roads being barely wider than one. In most areas, the towns lie close upon one another, so much so that they must be called New, Old, East, West, Upper, Lower, Little, or Big Whatever in order to avoid confusion.

Whatever monotony the repetitive town names cause is more than made up for by the lovely break that cycling through them provides during any long pedalling session. Hills, when they do occur (at least in these reclining northern lands) are more like gentle friends, urging you on although you might be a bit tired. Experienced tourers can take on their more fiendish and aggressive southern Alpine relatives, always ready to see you cough up a lung on the way skyward and emit a death rattle as you careen back down some mountain at breakneck speed. As long as one stays out of their clutches, cycling in most of Europe is a particularly easy experience. Bicycles in Europe also represent the pinnacle of the poor student's transportation triangle, the other two corners being public transportation and walking.

Public transportation is the least preferable option. Not only does it lead to many delays as German efficiency slowly takes its last gasps, it is an overall unenjoyable experience of extreme closeness with strangers. Especially during rush hour, it is not unlike taking a public bath, if you are lucky enough to find a seat. Otherwise, it is more like taking a public shower.

Walking, although enjoyable, is painfully slow and will not help you cover any appreciable distance in a day, even in the relatively close quarters of Europe. I enjoy walking, but walking from my out-of-the-way dorm to my out-of-the-way school takes exactly the same amount of time as it does for one artery to harden. Walking is just not a viable option for getting around Europe. That leaves the bicycle, which thankfully is completely practical 9.3 times out of 10.

I am not the first person here to think so. German innovator Karl Drais invented the bicycle while living in Mannheim and took the first two-wheeled tour ever, from Mannheim to a coach inn not far away. Drais actually kind of walked there on that first bicycle (it had no pedals). It was actually a kind of running machine that supported you with its seat while you propelled it forward with the same system used in Fred Flintstone's car.

Of course I have bicycles at home in Canada, but like everything else I have stored away over there, they are useless to me in my current location. Now, as an exchange student on a budget, I am obliged to go out and acquire yet another bicycle but must do so as cheaply as possible. Since free is the best sort of cheap, I will aim first in that direction. If necessary, I will break down and buy a bicycle, but I can't see how that will be necessary in Germany.

Fortunately for me, the wastefulness of a rich, Western, consumer-driven country like Germany, combined with the laziness of most foreign students who live in dorms like mine, provides a near perfect storm for someone looking for a free (although always slightly broken) bicycle. I am sure that this picture repeats itself in every housing or apartment complex that has a high turnover of residents. When our students only stay for a semester or two, they simply ditch their bikes when leaving, especially because nobody wants to purchase what is usually a somewhat broken bicycle.

Broken bicycles are actually a bit of a problem here. They tend to accumulate in the bike room until you can't get in or out of the thing with a working bike you wish to store there. Then, the building manager (the Hausmeister) eventually gets around to tagging derelict bikes, and if the owners don't fix or remove them in 30 days, he trashes them.

This is great. Unfortunately, all of the broken and unwanted bicycles from my building are locked up and controlled by the world's laziest, noncommittal, and (I think) manic-depressive Hausmeister. (Still, it would be through him that a whole series of free bicycles would eventually come into my grasp, albeit at the price of Herculean effort on my part.) This is how it all came together.

One day in the building where I live, a notice went up on the basement bike room door. This notice said, in effect, that the Hausmeister had amassed a large pile of broken and abandoned bicycles that had been cluttering up the bike area for the past few months. From this date forward, he would keep the offending bicycles on hand for a maximum of 30 days, after which he would send them to the tip. As these bikes were all somewhat broken or had been left behind by already departed former students, it seemed fairly likely that, in a month's time, the Hausmeister would still be sitting on most of this El Dorado of bent and broken bikes.

Eureka! Eventually, it would be from this pile of parts that I would assemble my European exploration bicycle. All I had to do was find a way to broach this delicate matter with the Hausmeister. Ironically, that would turn out to be the easy part. Finding the Hausmeister would turn out to be much more difficult.

Even the most conscientious German Hausmeister is known to be a rare animal to come across in its natural surroundings, otherwise known as the building for which he is ostensibly responsible and in which he should normally be present and accounted for. Some even live in the building they care for, but German Hausmeisters are usually busy but part-time professionals who take care of buildings on the side while they have much more lucrative and important main jobs elsewhere as tradespeople, handymen, or used appliance repair people. Worse still is if the Hausmeister has another building or two in his stable of after-hours jobs. Most seem to, and then they are really difficult to cross paths with. The lure of easy money (getting paid, however small an amount, to care for a building you practically never visit, is an irresistible inducement to most Hausmeisters) sucks them down this path. A Hausmeister will commit to take care of another building, and then another, and so on, until the pressure of the responsibility (although not the actual labour) forces him to give up such demanding obligations and go on paid sabbatical so he can soothe his strained nerves.

All of this means that you might rarely if ever catch a glimpse of the Hausmeister assigned to your building, and if the garbage gets taken out at all or the windows cleaned, you will start to believe that there are such things as helpful elves or benevolent forest creatures who work on your behalf while you sleep, because no mortal could do all this whilst staying invisible.

All this lack of seeing your Hausmeister might have you doubting his very existence, despite the show of giving him an office, posting his office hours on its door, leaving a mobile phone number where you can leave him a message, or other contrivances.

So, simply reaching the Hausmeister is hurdle Number 1 in any task, and it is kind of a prerequisite to the task of acquiring a free bike. Convincing him to hand over said bike will be Job 2, but a piece of cake in comparison: no Hausmeister with between 30 and 50 leftover and rotting bicycle carcasses can object to having someone come by and offer to take a few of them off his hands. Plus, I will be recycling them back into going concerns. How could anyone look askance at that?

Despite the vast amount of litter that sometimes chokes the streets here, Germans have a reputation for being environmentally friendly, recycling loving, not-messy people. And since Hausmeisters are known to hate actual work and should be more than happy that a person would come around and relieve them of even one ounce of it, the idea of taking a few heavy objects off their plate should come as a welcome surprise. If I took even three bikes off the pile (to make one good one), that would be like carrying away 10% of the pile for him (all figures estimated). I would be whisking away an ominous black cloud of bother. How could he not want this? How could the idea fail? And how could this idea not occur to more people, so that there were no broken bicycles unclaimed after the 30-day waiting period?

It turns out that in Germany, there is a completely and utterly and obviously reasonable way in which this solution would not occur to anybody else. It lies in the extreme and sacred division of labour and specialization of an individual's work and duties that rules over German industry and leaves virtually no room for ideas that are in any way outside the framework of normal everyday operations. Anyone who does so, or even floats an idea for doing so, is looked upon with scorn, like a strikebreaker who has just placed a foot over a picket line. In this case, the Hausmeister would have a certain procedure in mind for what to do with these bicycles, even if actually doing it was the last thing he wanted to do (work-wise or environmentally), but his upbringing and his training will hardly let him do anything else. Thinking outside the box is not valued when people think there is only a lonesome desert outside the box.

What normally happens in a case like this is that the Hausmeister first puts that notice on the bicycle itself. Any broken or even unused bicycle he finds lying around in his domain is subject to this. This notice informs the owner that, if nothing changes, the bicycle will be forcibly removed after 30 days. The Hausmeister then removes the offending bikes and builds a large pile of them somewhere else, to make room for functioning bikes to take up space in the bike room and on the bike racks outside the building.

This pile is then subject to another 30-day holding period of its own, when the notice on the bike room door is in effect. After that second 30-day period, the Hausmeister calls a scrap metal handler, who comes and gets the pile and takes it away.

My building has a large, unused backyard attached to it, but my Hausmeister decided to lock our party room and dump all of the broken bikes in there. Although that might seem ineffective in itself or to circumvent, bend, or break some other rule of procedure of how to treat the party room of building you manage, I can assure you it does not. In fact, it makes perfect sense to the Hausmeister. If he were to simply pile the bikes outside, who knows what would happen to them? And he is responsible for them for the next 30 days while errant owners might actually come by to claim one or two of them. Scavengers might pick through such an exposed pile and make a mess of it while it is awaiting further professional attention, processing, and eventual pickup. No, this would not do.

And what if the pile were so reduced (by scavengers, for instance, or neighbourhood people looking to repair or improve their own bikes) that the scrap metal dealer who had been called to pick up the pile in 30 days had less to deal with than planned? How could the Hausmeister explain to him that there had been a change in the number of bicycles and that he should bring a smaller trailer, or that all that remained were two seats and one set of handlebars? The scrap metal dealer's time would be wasted, his hopes dashed, his trailer brought in vain. No, this would never do.

And because no building has space to house an indoor bicycle dump for 30 days, our party room was sacrificed for this purpose. This does perfectly. It makes sense. Students can easily gather elsewhere.

But that second notice, the one on the bike room door that gives a second 30-day period, is pointless. It does say that, if you have suddenly noticed the disappearance of your bicycle but seem to recall it had a flat tire, a rusted chain, or looked like it had not moved for the past 15 years, you could reclaim it simply by alerting the Hausmeister. But who does this? Anyone who finds their bike missing is already an anomaly. Perhaps they just returned from a one-year overseas exchange such as I am on. Even if they did, they would never in their lives be able to find the Hausmeister. He is much too smart and wily for this to happen. The second notice is merely a formality and the way things have always been done.

So up goes the notice and down starts the count, and the bicycles block the party room for a month. After the first 30 days begins an indeterminate period in which the pile of bicycles just sits, the twisted frames settling together like an ugly, metal Jenga while the Hausmeister ostensibly organizes the orderly removal of said pile via a man with a trailer.

But this doesn't just happen. Sixty days have already passed in the official enterprise, and now more days are ticking away since the expiration of the second notice because the Hausmeister is AWOL. It could be any number of days before he reappears, probably greater than 10 but less than 365 because that is when there will be a new crop of abandoned bikes to deal with.

In this slow and painful way both innovation (the idea of building new bikes from old) and the bicycles themselves go to die in Germany, killed by this extreme but coveted job specialization and its finest proponent, the absentee, labour-averse Hausmeister.

All of this procrastination requires real work. A Hausmeister's goal in life is to appear to be busy, if he appears at all, and to avoid ever having to be forced to reveal the tangible results of any of his travails, even if threatened with torture most vile. Again, this depends on the Hausmeister, but this is the quality level we get in the place where I have been living.

Appearing busy did not seem to be my Hausmeister's goal, because that requires appearing. Why would he want to go to all the trouble of feigning busyness, in plain view, by putting in a performance worthy of a professional actor when all he was being paid was a Hausmeister's salary? Actors make good money, don't they? Our Hausmeister, rather than go through the work of putting on such an elaborate and demanding show, simply dispensed with the show altogether. What a stroke of brilliance! This sole manoeuvre meant the Hausmeister could simply not be found no matter how hard one might have been looking for him. He was thus able to stealthily keep his exact whereabouts unknown and make everyone start to question his very existence. He could hide in this way right through his supposed office hours and for several weeks on end completely avoid me. I could not find heads or tails of him.

Sometimes he was sick, he said, but then he somehow hauled himself across town to post a notice to that effect in our building. Sometimes an assistant would appear but, not being fully versed in the ways of the Hausmeister, could not perform any of the necessary tasks or repairs. In that sense, the assistant acted as nothing more than a talking notice, repeating the same basic information that the Hausmeister had posted.

Once, an assistant even told me that the Hausmeister was sick but would be returning on Monday. On Monday?

Now that was real news! How could one know, when sick, that one would no longer be sick and could return to work on Monday? The efficiency of such a system is astounding. It seemed like the first groundbreaking skill our Hausmeister had demonstrated, something not everyone could do, given the normal, unpredictable nature of illness.

The foretold Monday appeared and, lo and behold, so did the Hausmeister. I was still in awe of that fact when I checked to make sure that the pile of bicycles was still present, so that my taking up a little of his precious time discussing them would not be in vain. I passed by his open office door and stuck my head inside far enough so that even the most violent gust of wind could not accidentally slam it shut on my possibly only chance.

The Hausmeister apparently was on a break, after having just arrived for work. He sat at his desk doing nothing, apparently overcome either with the sheer joy of having survived his recent illness or with the horror of the pile of work and requests that had collected on the desk in front of him, or mentally plotting his next plan of escape. When he looked at me, I detected a further note of sadness, like a deer caught in the headlights that suddenly recalls what headlights are attached to, and I felt a tinge of sympathy for this poor creature, pathetically but conveniently trapped by my presence in his doorway. I was moving in for the kill.

He clearly noticed this predicament. Just moments after sitting down to start work, and just as he might have been heading out to enjoy his first cigarette or sandwich of the day, there I was. What could explain this? There was no escaping me now, for the office only had one door, and I was wedged in it, and the sole window was too small for my bulky Hausmeister to ever think of wriggling through.

But a seasoned Hausmeister's cunning knows virtually no bounds, and this one did not need to escape the physical confines of this small room to elude me. He simply said, when he regained his senses, that he was far too busy on this first day back to deal with human inquirers at this time. Far too many pieces of paper had built up on his desk during his absence, and he would have to deal with these first. I could come back during the next office hours, if I liked.

I told him what I wanted anyway, just to put him in the right frame of mind for my next visit, but this set him back to his glassy-eyed reverie from which he had just emerged. This only lasted a few seconds while he pondered the fairly simple request. Extraordinary, astounding maybe, but simple. Anyhow, it fazed him only shortly. He was soon again hail and hardy, waving me away with a, "Kein Problem" (no problem) and a reminder to come back another time.

Office hours are only on Mondays and Thursdays, so right there the Hausmeister had bought himself at least three days during which I feared the pile of bicycles might be shifted at any moment. I had to wait the bulk of a week to see the Hausmeister again. All I could do was check on the pile every day.

When Thursday came, the Hausmeister didn't. He sluffed off those office hours, but somehow I managed to catch him, again with his office door carelessly left open, a few days later. Now I didn't care how he felt; I was going to ask him again, damn him. This random and out-of-the-blue visit really moved me up the ladder of bothersome and perplexed my Hausmeister fully. He pulled out another weapon: he pretended not to know me or remember what I had wanted earlier.

Funnily enough, so much time had passed since our last meeting, this was almost plausible. I have to admit, I hardly recognized him either, his absences having grown so long and regular. I had a little trouble being absolutely certain this was the same Hausmeister I had spoken to earlier, but I pressed on anyway. Something about the unique wobble of his second chin made me feel certain that I had the right man. I explained the whole thing again.

"Ja, ja," he said. Why not? That makes perfect sense. After all, the bicycles are still there and to be frank, are more trouble than they are worth, but then again, isn't also, say, a broken refrigerator or a flooded washroom? The bicycles were just sitting there, yes, going to waste.

I could see them any time I liked... provided I made an official appointment first.

Oh, this guy was good.

I was standing right there in the door of his office, which is located directly across the hall from the entrance to the party room, but getting him to cross that hall would require an appointment. He was really good.

We settled (thankfully) on the next afternoon and went our separate ways. I don't know why I felt that this time he would make it, but I guess I was falling back on the saying that when a German makes an appointment, 9 times out of 9.78 times, he keeps it.

Tomorrow afternoon came, and so did the Hausmeister. He even had tools I could use to disassemble the bikes as needed. I could go at the pile as long as I kept it somewhat neat and orderly, and I could take as many bicycles as I liked.

Then he added that, if I should happen to find a bike that, without too much work, might suffice to serve his wife for short rides around their weekend home (their weekend home?!) well then perhaps I could do that one up also, because it would be a shame to waste another bike that might be so easily repaired but in which I was not personally interested. This guy was really, really good.

He then unlocked the magical storehouse of bikes, handed me the tools, and told me again that any passable bike would do for Mrs. Hausmeister, and left me to it.

Then I stood before an immense pile of bicycles, as big as a mountain of rubbish during a garbage strike. I dug in and got started. Not only did I have to find and build a decent bike for myself, I now felt duty-bound to provide one for the little woman in the Hausmeister's life. What could I do? The Hausmeister had one-upped me again. I felt like a small parasite that inexplicably had found itself with a much larger parasite attached, sucking the life out of it. Mr. Hausmeister (in his esteemed opinion, surely) had already completely exceeded the call of duty for me. It seemed only fair that now that he had taken all of five seconds to unlock a door for me that I should invest the next God knows how many hours of my life building a bicycle for his missus, if at all possible, when I had done all of this work simply to get myself to the point of building one for myself.

In the end it was worth it, though. After an eight-hour marathon of lifting, sorting, sifting, weighing, measuring, and comparing bicycle components, I had pieced together two good, solid bicycles for myself, as well as a purple Frankenstein of a child-sized mountain bike for what I was hoping was a rather small Hausmeister's better half.

I took my two new bicycles to my room for safekeeping and left the other one propped against a column in the middle of the party room for the Hausmeister to find.

A few short days later the pile was gone, and so was the Hausmeister and his purple bicycle. Without a word (to me, anyway), the Hausmeister had left his position with the building and gone on to easier or greener pastures, probably, where the residents of the building would be less demanding or less physically present, like a morgue or a night shift at a car dealership.

I felt very lucky to have gotten my bikes when I did. Not long afterward, another student searching for a bike was disappointed to find how expensive they were in these parts and chose to rent one of mine for the month he had left in Germany.

Unfortunately this student later brought back my bike with enough damage to wipe out his rental price and the time I had spent building it, and I will have to invest more time and now money, finding parts to repair it. Slow

Ignacio, from Chile, will never be totally forgotten for this.

The new Hausmeister is strangely present, a veritable whirlwind of (so far) useless energy. He is looking into fixing our broken bathroom light (we have been showering – and worse – in the dark for a few months now). He is investigating replacing our broken refrigerator (the previous Hausmeister's inquiries did not lead to an intervention and therefore we still have warm food even when it is meant to be cold).

He is busily taking notes on various building deficiencies on the same ineffectual clipboard as his predecessor used, weighing and sifting who would be best to call to fix a particular problem and how much it might cost and when it could best be done, given holidays and availabilities and other work that would need to be done first by these contractors at other buildings in this and other cities.

He dolefully shakes his head at the very mention of items that need attention and slowly writes them down, but to date, not one thing has actually been repaired.

Nothing at all has changed except that I have one and a half good bicycles with which to enjoy the good weather and good landscapes of Europe, whenever either of them should put in an appearance around here. Until then, I have time to fix that bicycle.

Like A Ripple Outwards

Mannheim might not be an art capital of Europe, but it is the perfect place from which to embark on any art travels, being so centrally located. It truly is the perfect place for me, in that sense.

I have had a train pass for the local region since arriving here, which means that I can pretty much travel anywhere within an hour or two of my city without paying anything extra. And now that I have a bicycle, I feel it is really time to start exploring the local region. I can even take the bicycle on the train to the edge of my travel zone, then ride off to wherever I like, then cycle back into the zone and catch a train home.

Obviously what I want to see is the art, and guess what the problem with that is? It is everywhere. There is way too much of the stuff here, so I really don't need to go far at all to start seeing it. After viewing what is on hand in Mannheim, I can head out in virtually any direction and run into staggering amounts of Kunst (art) no matter where I look.

Our famous neighbour, Heidelberg, is the obvious first stop. At only 24 kilometres away, it can be reached in about 15 minutes by train (plus the much longer time it takes to get yourself to the station and wait for the train to arrive). On the Heidelberg end, the city centre is another 15 or so minutes from the train. It all adds up. By bicycle, the trip is virtually just as fast, at just over an hour, so I have done both.

Heidelberg clearly has its attractions and points of touristic interest. Many visitors swoon over the supposed beauty of its position on the river and its romantic castle ruins high above, but to me, Heidelberg is not all that. It is okay as a tourist trap and maybe even for everyday living right next door to my city, but I don't feel that it is the tourist Mecca that people make it out to be. Some of its most interesting points-of-interest aren't even tourist attractions at all.

Up the decidedly touristy Philosophenweg (the philosophers' way), a famous and popular path that leads up the Heiligenberg mountain across the river from Heidelberg proper, you can find the abandoned and largely forgotten remains of the Thingstatte amphitheatre, a large structure built in 1935 by the Nazis using forced labour (they started early with this particular kind of pay scale). It is something to think about, that this site is lurking, literally buried in bushes, just outside the walking endurance range of most tourists who make the climb to snap pictures of the city.

This kind of thing is not necessarily submerged just beneath the surface of every similar tourist town in Germany, but it is in many. The Nazis were in power for so long, so forcefully, and so recently, that their history still hangs in the air in many cities and towns here.

In the art world, that history still haunts Mannheim, as we learned, and it haunts Heidelberg, too, but in the strangest places. Back down the hill, and after a 30- or 40-minute walk toward town, the intrepid visitor can find a museum tucked away into a corner of a nondescript building no tourist would spend a moment contemplating. This museum has an unfortunate connection to that political (and non-wage paying) party ideology that did such a nice job putting together that amphitheatre up the hill.

This museum is on a quiet little side street and dates back over 100 years. It is stuck onto the end of the psychiatric clinic of the University of Heidelberg. Why the Nazi party would have been interested in a museum attached to a mental hospital will soon make itself all too clear.

The museum in question houses the Prinzhorn Collection (it is at Vossstrasse 2, in Heidelberg). The entrance price is a grand total of 2 Euros (a complete bargain in the world of continental museums). Ironically, this is the only fee-charging museum that ever let me in for free when I told them that I was studying art history.

The Prinzhorn Collection is made up entirely of art created by mental patients from this and other German psychiatric hospitals. It dates far enough back to have an extensive collection of art made by patients from the time around the First World War so that, when the Nazis started thinking about it, it was the perfect place to get art with which to compare and denigrate the best Modern Art of the day (when the Nazis got that on their minds).

You see, the Nazis were planning (and held) a 1937 exhibition of what they called 'Entartete Kunst' or, roughly, degenerate art. The Nazis rounded up thousands of paintings from world-leading artists and museums in Germany (the Nazis did not like what they were seeing at the time in German museums and galleries), in order to plan a show that would demonstrate their distaste for the art of the day and show a more acceptable style of art they were interested in propagating. Modern Art was not the direction the Nazis wanted German artists to take. Any art that did not particularly touch their fancy or help promote the company mission statement was thrown into the degenerate pot. That pot included pretty much anything (and anyone) you can think of in European art at that moment (many famous foreign artists were also working in Germany, had worked there, or had works hanging in German museums and galleries). The Nazis then cunningly found a way to try and make that art seem ridiculous or spurious: they rounded up another (although much smaller) batch of art, all made by the certifiably insane, to hang pretty much cheek-in-jowl with the art they were trying to discredit, in a huge exhibition.

After a massive debut, the show travelled throughout the country to make sure that every citizen had a chance to see it and come to the same general conclusion on Modern Art as the ruling party had. This was meant to show that clearly offbeat – but supposedly sane, professional, or famous artists – were not producing anything better than untrained and certifiably insane people were.

The unwritten point of this was that perhaps both classes of artists needed to be locked up or barred from producing work in order to leave the space cleared for more pleasing and palatable artists. The Nazi party clearly saw Modern Art as artistic or visual torture for viewers and did not want them subjected to it.

But the show had a strange outcome, or at least we think it did. Now we believe that the show was quite successful in proving that art made by mental patients – people who are clearly in touch with the offbeat corners of their minds – is quite similar to art made by artists who, by force of will or nature, upbringing, study, or outside aids like drugs and alcohol, also shed off the conventions and restraints of everyday life and common thinking to express themselves differently through art.

In the end, 70 works were taken from the Prinzhorn Collection and hung alongside those of the great artists of the day. Viewers were asked to distinguish which were the degenerate artists' and which were the mental patients', and (although it might have been propaganda) viewers said they couldn't tell. Hopefully some of the patrons of the time saw through this ruse and also enjoyed the insane art, because it was quite a coup for the creators of those pieces to have their works hung alongside the geniuses of the day, and I hope some viewers got that. Those institutionalized artists also produced some pieces that an average collector in our time would be proud to own.

Most of the works I saw inside the tiny museum (and it is tiny) were quite amazing. Possibly due to having such a small display space, most of the works that were on show when I visited dated from somewhere near the beginning of the 20th century, and most were from around 1907 to 1919. In case you never get a chance to go there, you can check out whatever you like from the collection just by searching for the Prinzhorn Collection online.

The guidebook that is on hand features some absolutely stunning works by, for example, Hans Karl Hohler (pseudonym Pohl), from around 1909 to 1916, one titled *Untitled (Allegory of an artist)*, a pencil and crayon drawing on paper. Another piece, by Emma Hauck, a 1909 pencil on paper work titled *Untitled (Letter to my husband)*, looks like she wrote the same piece of correspondence 100 or more times on the same piece of paper, until the entire page is nearly black with her handwritten message. The words are almost entirely illegible, but you can imagine them being either an oft-repeated lament, a heartfelt apology, or both, the lines being so incessantly repeated and doggedly copied.

Adolf Schudel, from Schaffhausen (where there was another institution), lived from 1869 to 1918 and drew *Toad Pond at Full Moon* in 1907, another stunning pencil drawing. His *Step Path*, another pencil on paper drawing, is akin to a visual nursery rhyme. It is too detailed to attempt to explain, and looking back at my notebook, I see that all I wrote about it was, "Wow."

Schudel was obviously amazing, but strangely, in this category, you can't say who is head and shoulders above others. Many of the artists seem to be incredible. Still, Schudel has a certain something and seemed to know it: he was the only one of the artists on display here who included a copyright notice at the bottom of all of his works. His *Horses Feeding Time* from 1907-08 completely merits such a notice, though.

These kinds of artists, almost universally without training and – not coincidentally – operating from the exact place that most other artists have to strive to reach (their unconditional souls) have all left reality behind (or rationality, let's say, or their petty, everyday thoughts and pressures), are known in art history circles as 'outsider artists,' and their works can fetch the near-astronomic prices that the very worst kind of contemporary art can. That means, while nobody is going to pay millions upon millions of dollars for these works, there are people who are willing to pay hundreds of thousands of dollars, at least. And why not? These artists were doing (more than a hundred years ago) what contemporary artists are still just getting around to. Otto O., for instance, another Prinzhorn artist, has a piece called *Untitled (Two-Headed Man)*, a pencil drawing on quite a lengthy piece of toilet paper.

When I visited, the museum had a newspaper story hanging in the entrance, telling of how two pieces of art made by outsiders permanently locked up on the inside were being acquired by the collection to the tune of 150,000 Euros each.

The article concerned Adolf Wölfli, called the most prominent outsider artist in the world. The Prinzhorn was seeking funds to acquire two of his pieces from a dealer for 150,000 Euros each. (The article was published in the Rhein Neckar Zeitung on Mar. 5/6, 2011.)

I don't want to simply gloss over the question of what trained artists bring to the table that outsider artists might not, but those things are often largely matters of having broad educations, particularly in the humanities, or in art history or artistic technique. What outsider artists bring is what really makes art: the lives they lived, their sufferings, their own humanity, all of which apply or act in ways that truly make art.

I wonder what happened to all of these outside artists shown in the Prinzhorn Collection? They were certainly troubled individuals, difficult or misunderstood (or possibly misdiagnosed at that time). They were talented, that is sure. It is interesting that their works are so beautiful and not brimming with what we might think was going on in their minds: images of their confinement, disconnection from the world, their situations, dreams, nightmares. There are almost no images of anything negative, no pictures of death and destruction or latent memories. In fact, many of the images look like versions of paradise or other fantasy lands, as if being whatever these people really were (crazy, autistic, ADD sufferers, abuse survivors, who knows) relieves them of a lot of the stress and pressure of daily living or is, conversely, such a raw deal that all one can do is think about the opposite, about escape.

Only a few pieces are in any way disturbing. One piece, by Heinrich Lutz, from 1918 is a pencil and oil on paper drawing of an orgy, a literal tower of people fornicating, with many words written in the background, but that is about as serious as it gets: a picture of a lot of people who might actually just really be enjoying themselves is one of the most questionable pieces in the collection.

Disturbing, then, depends on your point of view, as well as your definition, kind of like Bill Clinton's definition of what the people in such a picture might really be doing.

There is obviously more to see in and say about Heidelberg, but other destinations beckon. In an ever-widening circle stretching outward from my base in Mannheim, there will be a mind-boggling number of things to see. Just as Heidelberg is only 15 minutes away, so are the imperial cathedrals at Speyer and Worms and a thousand other things, and because I have a rational mind and can't forget the pressures of daily life (and that this exchange is only a year long), I cannot seem to forget that time is ticking.

I Will Wear A Beret

I think one of the greatest, most powerful developments about coming overseas this year will be that it might be very freeing in a way. Europe is the home of the marijuana cafe, the hash brownie, more topless beaches than you can shake a stick and, well, other sorts of free-thinking things like that. I think I might be in need of some of this, strictly from a personal development standpoint.

I remember my mother reading all manner of self-help books meant to make her feel better about herself and her life, and I have read some, too. I never thought they helped enough, although they definitely made some difference. But you know what I mean: if we could all just eat our way slim or think and grow rich, we would all be slim and rich, wouldn't we?

My mother also loved inspirational slogans like, "When I am an old woman I shall wear purple," from a piece by English poet Jenny Joseph. Strangely enough, the last line from that poem is, "And make up for the sobriety of my youth." The first line was pinned up in our house as an inspirational message (not for me), but the last line (although I never knew it before) seems to fit me now more than I would ever have guessed.

Either way, I never thought much about the piece of poetry hanging on the wall, and I thought purple was a silly colour to wear unless you were in the business of being laughed at, but now I kind of sympathize with the idea of not being afraid of things like this.

I did not come here to discover this, but I found out quite quickly through doing so, that I have spent most of my life being afraid. That might sound strange, partly because most people think I am a confident and adventurous person, outgoing, and good with the public, but I think they are crazy. These people either have no clue about who I really am or don't know me at all, or I do have those traits, but they have nothing to do with the fact that I am still afraid on the inside.

When you start thinking about your fears, you will find you can categorize them and see what you are really afraid of, but it takes some doing, and the doing can take years. I always thought I was afraid of trying things, but I was wrong. More than anything, I think I am afraid of being embarrassed, but usually as the result of actually *trying*. It sounds simple, if a bit backwards, but believe me, it takes a while to see the difference between the two.

I have always been this way, and up until recently – not having recognized the cause – I haven't done much about changing that; I thought my young-self fears were something else. The true cause never entered my head. I still feel I have the mental age of a 19 year old, and when I was 19, I was utterly afraid of all sorts of things. Not common things like snakes or heights or airplane rides, but more esoteric things like dying before fame finds me or living in the town where I was born. I still don't want to do either of those things, but lately, coming here, I have uncovered what I really fear, that fear of embarrassment.

I should have gone somewhere years ago to test both my mental age and my fear level and then done it again later to see if one was going up and the other going down, to measure if I was making any progress in my mental life. People watch their weight and track their exercise or bank accounts but seldom do anything about checking their mental progress. I do the same.

So I have your usual garden-variety esoteric fears, then: fear of violence, fear of pain, fear of being wrongfully accused, fear of being convicted if rightly accused, fear of failing, fear of trying (in some cases, sure), fear of being bored, and that fear of being embarrassed. But the greatest of these is the fear of being embarrassed.

Somehow, someday, confronting at least some of these fears is going to be of paramount importance in my life. I can just feel it. Luckily, although I did not plan it this way, this might really be the whole point of a trip like this, although the enterprise raises fears of its own: the fear of going back to the same place after all this is over and falling right back into my old ways.

Largely, as we have heard all of our lives, getting over our fears often involves forcing ourselves to come face-to-face with them and then somehow conquering them. I have never had a problem coming face-to-face with my fears, but I don't recall getting over many of them. A dark alley is still a dark alley for me, even if I have walked down it a few times. It is just that I still walk down it in terror.

The experts say that we exhibit behaviours (such as fear) because we believe that we get something from doing it. We get something from not trying, from not going out on a limb. Probably safety. I don't know. I can't resist a shortcut, so I take the alley, but the whole time, I am hating it. I get the shortcut, but I don't get over my fear. What about speaking to a woman in a bar? I can't do that. In that case, I can't figure out what supposed benefit I am obtaining from not doing it. In that case, I think fear is simply sticking a toy gun in my ribs and robbing me blind.

Or, I might really, really be gaining freedom from embarrassment. And just such an epiphany occurred to me the other day. I did not seek it out, but perhaps it sought me. I was looking for something at the time, but not for an epiphany. After all, I was in a second-hand shop.

I am a frequent visitor to second-hand shops, and as you know, second-hand shops aren't in the business of selling epiphanies. Their standard merchandise, though, suits my budget, and I love making special finds there, usually far more interesting and unique things than you can get anywhere else.

My west-coast, Canadian psyche loves the recycling and

do-goodism associated with used stores, my collector's taste loves the forgotten and unloved treasures, and my fashion sense loves the Paul Smith jacket you bought for your husband, inexplicably thinking he would fit the same size he wore at your wedding.

This trip overseas has already yielded up some stunning second-hand store finds, although I have only found two or three such shops in my entire area. Most Europeans seem to find something slightly distasteful about reading other people's books or wearing their clothes.

One day, I had dropped into one of my favourite shops and was milling around in the absolute last resort, a kind of bargain-basement tent outside the building proper, where clothes go for their last chance at being adopted before they meet the shredder and end as mechanic's hand towels or carpet fibre. Most of the misfit clothing lurking in the bargain tent deserves this end.

But every once in a while a miracle happens, and that is what happened that day. Suddenly, I saw it. It was lying face up (I am not sure it even has a face) in a pile of gear from a bankrupt store or close-out sale gone wrong. It had somehow struggled its way to the very top of a heap of similar items and was lying on its back with its tummy exposed, trying to be noticed and begging to be picked up. It was no puppy, no animal, but it was made almost entirely from one: it was a 100% sheep's wool, navy blue, French beret, with a red lining and a lovely, embroidered label, totally authentic, hand-made in France, and waterproof.

I know that berets are not just French. They are actually a very international type of headgear. People wear them in many countries and cultures, but in most people's minds, I am pretty sure an authentic beret means a French beret, and this one was. Inside, on the carefully made label, it says, 'Splendid, pure laine, Impermeable, Fabriqué en France', pretty much what I said, but in French.

It was brand new and part of a load of unsold hats. I

was not sure why they were in the bargain tent. It was red-satin lined, had a brown leather headband, and the tiniest pigtail sticking out of its waterproof head.

The thing was fairly making my heart beat faster. Why was this pancake-shaped hat making such an impression on me? Why was I fascinated with all of its wondrous details? Hats have been a fear of mine for as long as I can remember. To be clear, I am not afraid of hats. I am not even afraid of wearing hats; I am afraid of what I look like in them. They look terrible on me, almost without exception, and when I put one on, I feel terrible about how I look with it on my head, and so I don't wear them. I simply don't have a hat head.

I wore hats when I was a kid. I have seen myself in them in old family photographs. They were always outlandish, to boot. They were never baseball caps or fedoras or something Johnny Depp would wear. They were always 10-gallon cowboy hats or sombreros or Indian headdresses. For someone who doesn't like the attention that wearing a hat brings, these iterations seem like strange choices to me now. Still, I guess at least some of them matched the cowboy boots, gun holsters, vests, or chaps I was often wearing in the same photographs from around the time I was six years old. I guess I was oblivious at the time, but since then, hats have become a horror for me. I guess I never developed that adult hat head that my younger self so glowingly promised.

I wore hats if I had to (like a beekeeper would), seldom in public (hiking in the woods or driving towards the blazing sun), and never as a statement of any kind. But I also know that I have, at the back of my mind, always thought about doing it. I have always wished that I could wear a hat with wild abandon. I think, if I had had the ability to wear hats, if I could really have pulled it off on a regular basis, where could I be now? What could I not have done with my life? As it stands, many doors were closed to me, all because of my lack of a hat head.

Professional bicycle racer? Hat. Downhill ski racer? Hat. Pilot? Hat. Captain? Hat. Astronaut? High-tech hat. Baseball player? Cowboy? Fireman? Chef? I had to avoid all of those professions just to avoid the hats. And yet this beret, innocently lying there biding its time, exerted an unusual and powerful force on me. In some sort of mystical, out-of-body experience, I saw my hand stretch out and reach for this blue beret, drift slowly closer to its upturned rim, and finally pick it up.

The beret seemed to shimmer in a navy-blue pool of sunlight. My hand felt the wooly goodness of it, as if angels had shorn it from the wool of 1000 heavenly sheep. I looked at it more closely. There were numbers inside the band that my addled brain could not comprehend: 59 and then 9 1/2, neither of which were North American enough for me to understand (I think my hat size is 7 3/4 inches; who knows what that even means here).

Not knowing exactly why, I lifted the beret off the pile and began to raise it upwards. Was I going to put this thing on my head? What for? Before I could answer those questions, the beret sucked down perfectly onto my dome. The thing fit me like a glove. What was I doing? I didn't dare look in the mirror; that would break the spell for sure. No, I thought, if this is fate or something like it, then it is meant to be. If the angels who shore those sheep and passed the wool to other angels who made this beret so that it could find me at this moment in time and win a new home for it on my hatless head, then who was I to tear all that asunder? The only thing for me to do would be to enquire about the price.

Knowing pretty well the intimate workings of the bargain-basement tent, I wasn't bound to be shocked at the asking price, even if there was a load of new hats sitting by it, as unusual as that was. It turned out the beret was selling today (and today only) for the princely sum of 1 Euro. Without so much as a thought as to where or when I would ever wear the thing, I plunked down the coin and became the proud new owner of an almost new hat.

You have to admit that the magic of the beret is that, if you really don't know where and when you might ever wear it, at least it offers you a zillion possibilities as to how to wear it. A beret can symbolize a thousand different circumstances and moods. The problem is finding a circumstance or mood you want to be associated with while wearing it. Circumstances like 'in public' might not be a first choice, nor would 'near home,' 'at work,' or 'at your own wedding.' A beret is just too powerful, too opinionated for most people to deal with right out of the gate (and here I mean both the wearer and the audience).

And moods? What are you trying to display? Rebel leader? Angry young man? Unpublished poet? Misunderstood painter? What do you want to be that could possibly be associated with a beret? The irony here is that, whatever it is, you can be much more easily associated with it in a beret.

People need time to get used to berets in general and to you in a beret in particular. A beret is not a starter hat. In a complicated metaphor, a beret would be the bigger fish when you still have smaller fish to fry. The feat of seeing yourself hatted should not be of paramount importance in your life or lead to heart palpitations. If it does, then you clearly have actual larger fish to fry.

So this is what I settled on: I would wear my beret but not in public or at least not in the beginning. And then later, I would wear it outside but nowhere near where I lived. I would, in the future, hopefully never wear it to work. The problem seemed solved.

A few reasons for this strategy have nothing to do with embarrassment. Regional and cultural issues also need to be considered. A beret might be incredibly international, but not everybody sees it that way, the Germans probably first and foremost. Years ago, the standard German hat assortment might have included the beret, but the current ones are the goat herder's mini fedora or the northern fisherman's cap or a plain, old, North American baseball cap. Nobody wears a beret around these parts unless he is looking to stand out or is a house painter with delusions of grandeur.

My decision about where and when I could appropriately don the beret left me with few choices. I started wearing it in my dorm room, but that was pretty timid. There was no Mediterranean sun on my face, no Mistral wind in my hair, no sailing down tree-lined lanes with a four-foot-long baguette strapped to the rear luggage rack of my bicycle. I needed more, and I needed it soon, like an addict. I tried the beret at different rakish angles, still in front of my mirror. I tried it at different depths. A beret can barely touch your head, just seeming to float above it like a felt crêpe, or you can squash it down so that the band descends either over or under your ears. You can push it so far to one side, so far back, or so far forward that you could wear it for three consecutive years as part of a Halloween costume and nobody would know it was the same costume. A beret doesn't look like much, but it can keep the rain off your head and even off your glasses.

In my travels, I did see a few beret-wearing men on the streets of Germany, but I did not garner much hope from them. They were all peculiar men. I saw a short man with a particular-shaped head, somewhat like a lightbulb. He wore his beret pushed all the way back, and by this I mean near vertical and it clung there, but when I tried this, my beret would simply slide to the floor.

After some time getting used to wearing the beret around my room, it was time to try wearing it outside, in the big, bad world from which it had come. This, clearly, for my level of confidence in hat wearing, could not be in Germany. For this, I needed to go to France.

Luckily, as students, we receive a regional train pass with which we can reach two cities just inside France. So one morning, my beret and I set off in the direction of one of them for a test drive under the open skies and approving gaze of its homeland.

On the way there, I simply carried the beret in my courier bag. Berets do no take kindly to folding, so it needed space. We rode secretly together on the two-hour train ride and slipped into France through its border city, Wissembourg, in late afternoon. There I tucked on the beret and headed into the great wide open, feeling fine.

I have to admit, a lot about France feels good. Something about the place just makes it a kinder, gentler sort of Germany. The change is immediately noticeable. Being that it is a border town, you might expect the place to exhibit less difference than a place deeper inside the country and further removed from Germany. Near the train station, which looks to be about 25 feet inside the country's boundaries, are the same stores we have in Germany. The train that brings you is German, but everything else is different.

In Germany, when you walk into the local supermarket, the cashier (or any other employee) barely acknowledges you. Eye contact is kept to a minimum. The cashier shoves your items across the scanner like an angry robot and demands the total. That's it. When I walked into the same chain of supermarkets in France, literally a baguette's throw from the border with Germany, the people inside greeted me with a hearty chorus of "Bonjour, Monsieur" and a "Comment-allez vous?" at the cash register, followed by cries of "Monsieur, monsieur, vos achats!" when I walked away, completely dazed, without taking any of my purchases with me.

I don't know for sure, but I don't think that all of this familiarity and friendliness can be ascribed simply to my wearing the beret. No, I think the people in France simply believe that life is beautiful and, at that moment, I agreed with them. It was simply a damn fine day to be in France wearing a beret.

And the rest, as they say, is history. I made the rounds of the historic city, dropped into stores and greeted people who either nodded or greeted me first with that same kind of wild abandon, stopped and took photos of the sites and canals and ruins, tried to direct some Asian tourists who obviously thought I knew my way around these parts, had something to eat, and then headed back for the train ride home. The day was a complete success. I felt wonderful.

But one short trip, despite the progress it showed, can't change me into a hat-wearing man in one go. It can't eliminate my fear of embarrassment just like that. It will take more practice than this, so the beret had to go back inside the bag for the ride home. I thought about wearing it and how much of a victory that would be, but I wasn't ready, despite the gathering darkness outside. I was headed for my rather large city. It was anonymous enough. I hardly ever run into anyone I know there, but on the other hand, if I were ever to encounter someone I knew, it would be there, and although the chances were slim, I didn't want to risk ruining the otherwise perfect mission so far. But still I thought, why can't I wear the beret until I get back to my room? Somehow I couldn't, but I was half okay with that.

Then, just after stepping off the train back home in Mannheim, all my fears were vindicated. Steps outside the railway station at the streetcar station, I caught sight of a fellow student. Seth was from the United States, probably the second-least beret-appreciative country on earth. I was not sure how he would take the sight of me in my beret. And to top it off, he was not alone; he had someone in tow.

I knew that his girlfriend and his parents were in town for a visit. I had not met any of them, so I could not be entirely sure, but there was a somewhat shorter girl near him (I am going to say at his side), and then, immediately behind him, two little people. At least, I believe that is the currently accepted expression for very, very short people.

When I saw these little people, well, yes, they looked like midgets to me, and moving through the crowd milling around the train and streetcar stations, they clung to Seth's trail like small sticky notes. I was already a bit bewildered that I had nearly run into someone I knew while debating about whether or not to don my beret. It was a mere stroke of luck that my more cowardly side had won that argument just moments before, and I had not been seen. I didn't really have time to process what I was seeing, but it certainly seemed to be three short people and one normal-sized Seth leading them somewhere.

I looked away in the hope that Seth would not see me. Staring at someone usually makes them return your gaze, and I didn't want that. At the same time, with my own beret misgivings running through my head, I suddenly thought, maybe other people also have their own secrets and fears. Maybe Seth was just as shy about introducing people to his Oompa Loompa parents as I was about wearing my beret in public. If I had had to deal with such a thing, too, it might have put my beret fears into perspective, but we can only worry about so many things at a time, it seems.

I was still not sure what I had just seen, and now, looking away, I only had my memory to rely on. I thought I would just get on the streetcar, facing away from the little group I had just seen, and hope for the best. I was not wearing my beret. Seth had no idea I had it, so it now seemed to me that if we met, he would be on the worse end of it, having to explain his tiny parents, and I didn't want that. I just wanted to get back to my room and celebrate my getaway. Meeting Seth would disturb the whole balance.

Seth's crew got on at the rear of the streetcar, and I hoped that just the sight of my back or my mannerisms would not be enough to give me away. I did wonder if I had some kind of crazy hat hair I wasn't aware of. Barring that, I had gone unnoticed and unembarrassed as of yet, did not have to tell anyone the story of where I had been that day, and was almost on the point of relaxing completely, despite the presence of Seth and his tiny troupe, when the train stopped at the next station, and my world was again threatened with change.

You could not make up the following details if you were the highest-paid television writer: at that stop, in walked another tiny human pulling a squeaky, wheeled shopping cart. He fairly waddled under his own weight and had to turn again and again to yank the recalcitrant cart a few more inches forward and between other people standing in the car.

In a kind of slow-motion sequence, this little man wheezed and waddled and wrangled his cart the three or four feet from the door to the empty seat beside me. Then he turned his backside toward the seat, put his tiny hand behind him on the seat cushion, and attempted to hop up and backwards into the seat. Three times.

I could not believe what I was seeing. I could not believe my luck or lack of it. I could not understand how or why there were suddenly so many tiny people in Mannheim. And why, if you were tiny, would you not get a better, more helpful cart? Surely Seth's parents would notice this noisy, hopping display and find this international counterpart irresistible. In their usual gregarious, American way, they would undoubtedly head up train or excitedly point him out to their son, saying, "Hey, let's go say 'hi' to him." Look, I don't know, but that is what I imagined would happen next.

My heart was beating in my ears, and I had to ride in that state, imagining things, frozen like a deer in the headlights of a miniature car, until my seat mate trundled out of the tram at the very next stop. He had made me endure less than 90 seconds of hell to save himself the 40-metre distance between stops, but quite rightly. His cart was obstinate. His legs were tiny. I felt terrible for being angry with him.

I jumped out at my stop, hoping Seth was no longer on the train (we lived in the same dorm) and had taken his tiny family somewhere, and I walked the three blocks home. Hours later and calmed by a nightcap, I enjoyed a return of the sense of pride I had felt earlier, although I no longer thought of the day as a total success, and my nerves were not quite back at 100%. I still felt that I had accomplished something and had looked quite dapper doing it.

I felt that I had somehow made a small dent in my fear of being embarrassed, although it will take much more than this to do anything lasting about it. But it was a baby step in the right direction.

I also realized something else. Thinking back, I was quite sure that Seth's parents were not midgets. At the exact moment that I had seen Seth and his petite girlfriend, they had been crossing the raised platform of the streetcar stop. His tiny parents, following behind, must therefore have been still standing in the lowered rail bed between platforms, ready to step up onto the platform with Seth. They were probably at least two feet taller than they appeared to be in the split second that I saw them, and because I had not looked again, there was nothing in my mind to confirm that at the time. So my short-people notions had set in, taken hold, and run away with me, much like my fears often do.

Maybe the moral of the story is that everything can, sometimes, use closer examination.

The Bulgarian Pig

First of all, let me say right off the bat, it is not my fault that this next story is about a Bulgarian student. I am sure that there are plenty of perfectly nice and clean Bulgarian students out there somewhere, possibly both at home and abroad, but the one I happen to live beside – and share a kitchen with – certainly isn't one of them.

This story isn't even so much about being clean. It is about not letting people's crap and their equally crappy attitudes just slide by. It is about figuring out what you no longer need to accept and not letting people off the hook too easily. I think I have been letting people off the hook for far too long, and this Bulgarian just climbed on and broke the camel's back.

To be fair, even this Bulgarian is probably a nice enough person. He probably just grew up in a way that taught him absolutely nothing about health and hygiene, let alone how to care for any kind of communal space. How to wash dishes or clean surfaces – or that those items might actually need such treatment in the first place – I now know are thoughts that have never crossed his mind. With so few people these days being raised by wolves, it is hard to imagine how a person can be indoctrinated into this kind of unsanitariness. Only two ways really come to mind: either he has a mother who does all of his cleaning for him so he has never had to experience it, or she is just as lousy at it as he is.

It is too bad, really. Everything else in my life is being cleaned up and organized nicely. But these are all fairly normal things for a communal students' kitchen. Nobody is really in charge. Nobody really knows who owns what, so people take it as a (false) sign that they are operating under anonymity. This makes them unnaturally bold.

The Bulgarian has been living next door for a year. I was here half that time and never put a face to the name on his door. All I knew about him was that he was contributing to the chronic mess in a kitchen shared by 10 people, and this was from hearsay. When he and most of the others went away for Christmas holidays (which lasts well into February), the kitchen was left in a sorry state. The three of us who remained put things back in order. Utensils were everywhere, garbage was all over.

I had not really used the kitchen, but I wanted to (I had not cooked in five months, due to the sad state of the place). With the mess makers gone, I decided that enough is enough.

A good example of the sanitary conditions our Bulgarian and others thought was perfectly acceptable was the refrigerator. When they went away, the fridge was in the same shape it had been in before they left, and the main problem was the spilled cream that had been left to congeal and yellow on the glass shelves. One of our residents liked to use cream on something, and in Germany, cream often comes in foil-topped plastic cups, like you might find yogurt in normally. Once you open one, there is no way to reseal it, and putting an open one back in the fridge is an invitation for trouble. The things fall over if you just look at them. Who knows who had owned the cream that didn't make it, but I threw away a good number of the corpses. Nobody made an attempt to clean the spills. The only proof we had that the cream lover still lived in the building was the regular reappearance of freshly opened cream containers. Lord, where do some of these people get their sense? If this is the summation of their moral compass of right and wrong as regards a fridge, how black their souls?

Of course, after seven of them had drifted back to their mothers, we noticed the change immediately: the people who made a practice of leaving piles of dirty dishes and putting their food wrappers on the counters and floors were evidently gone. Crimes against cleanliness had stopped. We now knew that the three remaining inhabitants were not the perpetrators, or they were waiting for the cover of the other seven's return to restart their misdeeds. The cream-loving fool was also truly well and gone during this period, so we survivors pretty much had our pool of suspects cornered. I think it was a bit more than coincidence that the three of us who remained did not have mothers we could conveniently go to and had thereby learned how to take care of some basic things in the kitchen.

I set about cleaning the kitchen. It was a huge task. The rotten food left over in the fridge went in the bin. The solid puddles of cream were scraped, soaked, washed, and finally subdued. And on and on.

Then, the most gruesome discovery was made: dirty dishes stored in a cupboard under the counter, happily giving birth to colonies of fungus, and a used and still-dirty frying pan on top of the upper cabinets, featuring a putrified glaze of oil and what once had been green onions. These two horrifying scenes baffled us. Had a student left some years ago without doing away with the utensils from his last supper? We discussed the find, but none of us could make sense of them. Even the Bulgarian – who, when on garbage duty did not take the garbage out for so long the other residents piled it in front of his door – wouldn't go this far, would he?

We threw away the dishes and soaked the frying pan to see if it could be saved, and the kitchen (although far from perfect) already felt, looked, and smelled better. And then the missing residents started to return.

The Bulgarian came first. I know this, because he was the first to knock on my door. I had never really seen or spoken to him in the preceding five months. He asked me who had cleaned the kitchen. I said I had. Oh, good, he said, because he was wondering where his plates had gone, although he had luckily found his frying pan in the sink.

I am sorry, I said. That was me. I chucked them. I mean, I threw them away. I have been around a lot, I added. You know? I have travelled a bit. I know people in different parts of the world go at things in different ways, but where, in the name of God, where people have learned to use knives, forks, and possibly even spoons, do people store dirty dishes with food in them inside the cabinets of their kitchens?? Oh, and then *leave* those kitchens and that food there to rot while they go off on their Christmas vacations??? This is, I said, one of those hypothetical questions, but it is worth an answer.

Oh, he sputtered, he leaves them dirty so that other people will not use them! Because nobody knows what belongs to anybody, nobody respects anybody's things. It was the only way he could keep his stuff out of the clutches of his fellow students.

I actually took a minute to pull myself back together after this answer, but I had a solution for him. I had spent some time during the clean up numbering the cupboards in the kitchen for this very purpose. There were tons of cupboards, but nobody could tell where they should put their belongings to keep them separate from everyone else's. I told him of this amazing new system and that, even without such a miraculous invention as numbered cupboards, leaving rotting food on dishes inside cupboards was not okay.

He was shocked at this, because people had been riding rough shod over his clean dishes for a year apparently, and this had been the best solution he had come up with so far. And now, the dishes he had so carefully saved were gone.

We had quite a heated discussion about it all, but in the end, all I can clearly remember (other than my quite graphic description of what larvae look like and how to tell the difference between fungus and mold) is that he said he would go out and buy some new dishes, and I remember feeling sure the exact same two fates would befall them: they would be left in some dark corner of his now-numbered cabinet space, complete with food scraps, and I would again dispose of them as soon as their whereabouts became known to me.

But don't think this was the end of it. After all, the kitchen had been far dirtier than just a set of rotting dishes. The very next day, I found food wrappers on the floor as soon as I stepped into the kitchen, and another portion of the same kind of wrapper on the counter next to a kitchen knife. I know, it was just two food wrappers, but we had had no wayward litter during the months during which only three of us had occupied the floor. Obviously one of our litter bugs was back in full force.

As befits my new style of kitchen management, I left a note pointing out the error. The very next time I saw the Bulgarian, he was peering at the note. I walked in and asked him if the wrappers were his. He said they were, and he picked them off the table and threw them in the trash. He said okay, he had made some mistakes, but a bit of messiness in a kitchen shared by 10 people was to be expected. Again, it took me a minute or two to digest this declaration.

I do not know if we are going to be able to reform him, to bring him into the modern world of garbage cans and cleaning sponges. I just don't know. He is young. It might be possible, but I am not holding out hope. And that doesn't really matter. The issue with this one student is not the issue at all.

What matters is figuring out how far we want to go to hold people's hands, or hold their crap up in front of their faces to make them see that what they are doing is unacceptable, because it takes work and is not pleasant. But we can't let everything slide. As much as I hate confrontation, I am starting to get new ideas about how much confrontation I can stand.

It is a tiny thing to confront someone about being a

semi-private public nuisance in your own kitchen. But think about it: if you can't confront people who are walking all over you in little tiny ways like this, how can you confront the people who are doing it in great big ways?

In that way, the Bulgarian Pig was another lesson I needed to learn.

The Struggle Bus

There are more problems in student life than dirty dishes and dreary accommodations. We should now move on to the real mover and shaker in a student's world: alcohol.

I already know that students drink. Before coming here, I was a student, having just finished a combination of four part- and full-time semesters, some while also working full-time. So I know about student drinking. It is just that, before coming here, I never had to live with other students who were drinking. I lived with a professor who was drinking, and let me tell you, that is not the same thing.

First of all, a professor who is drinking (I can almost guarantee you) is consuming much less alcohol than any student. She would be – volumetrically speaking – merely sipping when compared to the amounts most students pack away on a regular basis. They just don't need to. Professors (having once been student drinkers) have sponged in much more alcohol than most students ever will. Why? Because most professors went all the way to their doctorates, meaning they endured three distinct levels of university education before their student drinking days were over. That can add up to an impressive record of consumption.

Professors who are *still* drinking have discovered a thing or two about life and themselves: they have determined their optimum daily intake; they only exceed it on special occasions or when they feel they might finally reach some sort of job security; they can still perform all basic tasks like marking term papers when they drink moderately; life is a little bit nicer when they are drinking; and informal studies show that professors, when drinking, are willing to look a little more kindly upon the many small errors those term papers almost surely possess. The importance of this to many students should not be downplayed.

Students who are drinking, on the other hand, can do little more than sit around and – if awake – talk. This is, in a way, a sad reality, because it proves indisputably that students under the influence of alcohol cannot do anything more or better than when they are dead sober. This begs the question: what exactly do they get for their money? It certainly isn't a burst of energy. Maybe they are simply lazier than their professor forefathers. Professors, if allowed to go unchecked back to their student drinking levels, would surprise you with their levels of energy and propensity to go out and chant, wave protest flags, march in the streets, and overturn or burn cars.

But heavy student drinking, at least for international exchange students, cannot all be blamed on the students themselves. Part of the problem is in their title: international exchange. Probably the number one reason that exchange students drink so much (at least here in Europe) is favourable exchange rates. For many students, alcohol in their temporary home countries costs much less than it does in their real home countries.

Many countries grossly underprice their alcohol. Germany, where I am stationed, is particularly good at this. The people in charge of setting prices are either doing just as much drinking as the average student, imagine themselves to be everyone's benevolent if misguided uncle, or are woefully unaware of how much more their booze could fetch at retail. Potential profits slip through their fingers. Those faceless bureaucrats who make everything here function could charge three or four times as much as they do, and it still wouldn't make a dent in student consumption, especially if that student has a North American wallet. And herein I include my own poorly prepared wallet.

It is, by way of contrast, a crying shame what we must fork over for beer, wine, and spirits in my home country.

There, it is like we are trying to create some sort of class division between the haves and the have-nots at the very spot where no such distinction should be allowed.

In Europe, they realize quite rightly that booze is for everybody, even – sometimes – children. In Germany, a litre of imported French wine costs about 1.69 Euros, less than $3 back home at the current exchange rate. I never met a bottle of wine back home (and at home, that bottle would have been 750 ml, not a litre) that cost less than $7.99, more usually $10. In both countries, the quality of such low-priced (let's say bargain) wine is frighteningly low but also uncomfortably similar, considering the great price difference. At least in Germany, it is worth buying. Here, it serves its purpose: it is student wine, to be drunk while both you and the wine are young. In Canada, just because of the price, you would feel vindicated serving it to guests, although your guests might not agree.

The unfortunate thing is that, given these many advantages of being a moderate to heavy drinker in Europe, students go and waste the price per litre advantage by drinking far too many of those underpriced litres. They end up drinking the same dollar amount that they would if they had just stayed home in their own countries. They just end up drinking a lot more volume, and when they drink that much, they end up riding the struggle bus.

I first heard that phrase early one morning, when a few of our American students were slovenly boarding a bus for one of our trips. It was probably just a few hours after they had stopped drinking and gone to bed. They were feeling no love for the morning.

The struggle bus is, of course, no literal conveyance. It is not a vehicle you can drive, because driving it in that condition would be wrong. You can only ride the struggle bus, although some students hallucinate that they are driving it. It is a figurative creation, but to those who climb on board at the end of one of our nightly kitchen parties or shortly thereafter in one of the local clubs or bars or back in their own room, it seems literal enough. The struggle bus is what happens when, after a night of drinking, you have to get up and go to an early class at some ungodly hour (say, in the harsh glare of early afternoon). The whole experience, although named after a bus, is more like being forced to stare at a very bright light while somebody rhythmically taps your head with a sledgehammer. I am still not sure whether getting on or off the bus is the worse experience. For a long while here, I never personally got on the bus, but I knew plenty of people who did, and I was usually accompanying them somewhere at the time.

The main cause of the arrival of the struggle bus, as I pointed out, are the nightly kitchen parties in the student dorms. I arrived for this exchange a little later than the rest of the semester's cohort (although still plenty early, as classes would not start for weeks), and I quickly realized that the other students had already gotten a jump on me in the drinking arena. Most of them already had taken a trip or two on the bus we are speaking of. The bus was pretty much parked right outside their doors. They could give a pretty good description of it.

For every 10 dorm rooms, there is one large kitchen. Here everyone gathers to drink (pre-drink, actually) either as an end in itself or before going out to a club or bar or disco where drinks are far too expensive to enjoy, especially in quantity. No student can afford to start cold on a night of celebrating at a club, and no student wants to start at a club dry either. Kitchen parties help mitigate the risk of either folly taking place.

The one thing I learned right off the bat about kitchen parties is that they are not the kind of party I had been used to attending. That is not to say I had spent a lot of time going to parties in the past, but I do like to think I know what makes a good party or at least can recognize the difference between a good party and a chat. A party is where any number of wild and crazy things are likely to happen, where music (although good) can be blaring, where talking (even screaming) is often futile, and where people feel the need to crawl off into dark corners to communicate verbally or physically with one another. Nobody clings to anybody at a kitchen party; it is just talking.

A chat, on the other hand, is sitting around with your mates or members of the opposite sex, talking. Nothing more than that. You could do this anywhere, and to do so, you wouldn't need any alcohol. Sure, lots of chats take place in pubs, but at least pubs have some sort of ambience. A chat in a dirty kitchen, with alcohol, is just a waste of alcohol, and it is still just a chat in a kitchen. It is not a party.

But here alcohol is the party. It is the central figure in any party. My people here will even get together drunk, because some of them will pre-drink the pre-drinking. But the rest is just talk. It might sound like yelling or shouting or Spanish at times, but it is just conversation. I wonder: have they never seen one of their parents' house parties or seen a good one in a film? If they had, they would realize that our kitchen affairs are missing some essential party elements: we have no drag races, nobody gets unnecessarily or spontaneously naked, there is no groping (the lighting is really just too awful for that), and there are no games, bets, dares, or pranks. Nothing gets set on fire. Talk about needing an old radical to show you the ropes.

Once in a while there will be a killer game of beer pong or flip cups (if you don't know, don't ask, because you don't want to know what your kids are up to each time you leave the house for a few hours). Some of the people now in their second semester have become experts at either or both, and a few look like they have been playing since their early, early teens (I told you you didn't want to know). The games aren't that hard. You either throw ping pong balls into cups of beer that your opponent must then drink, or you rapidly drink a cup of beer and then set it (empty and upside down) on the edge of a table and flip it so that it stands up properly, and this continues relay style down the table (oh, now I've told you).

No matter what the night's entertainment will be, we go to these parties. The notice goes up online after school and we descend on one host's kitchen and proceed to turn it into a sticky bottle return depot. There is never food, although we always gather in a kitchen, and drinking that is uninterrupted by snacks is really quite effective.

But kitchen parties, in the metaphor of the struggle bus, are just transit buses, commuter lines. You don't really ride very far in a kitchen party. You get on and you wake up the next day not far away, possibly even your own bed. These are not 16-day European tours. For a true glimpse of what goes on inside the struggle bus, you really need to put on some miles, get out of town, and feel it zooming down an open road that, at the same time, is made up of nothing but hairpin turns.

The first opportunity I got to see the struggle bus in operation was on a trip to a nearby wine festival. Bad Dürkheim is a pretty little hamlet nestled up against the wine-growing hills of the neighbouring Pfalz region, about a 40-minute tram ride from Mannheim. The important part of that sentence was not that it is a pretty little hamlet in the region of Mannheim; the important part is that 40-minute tram ride. That is what sets the stage for the next part of this story.

Streetcars, unlike commuter trains that often travel over similar distances or for similar lengths of time, do not have washrooms. Unlike on a commuter train, 40 minutes (especially standing) on a packed streetcar can seem like an eternity. International students who have been pre-drinking up until a few minutes before such a streetcar whisks them off to a distant wine fest can sorely test the elasticity and holding power of even the most youthful bladder. I couldn't help calculating how much used alcohol we were internally carrying with us to this wine festival when we set off.

It was a hot fall afternoon when we tumbled out of the streetcar at our destination and lined up hopefully in front of a terracotta-army-sized collection of portable toilets, before heading on towards our reserved party tent space at the festival. We joined a flowing path of humanity, a moving carpet of people, all headed towards this tiny wine fest in the middle of nowhere. I was a little surprised that it would draw such a crowd, because when we got to it, it was nothing more than a slimmed-down version of Oktoberfest in Munich. It was much smaller than that epicentre of beer swilling, but the people were just as excited to be there.

There we drank and ate and watched a truly horrible band play American oldies for a crowd of mostly German oldies. How we got booked into that tent I will never know. It must have been the only thing left at last minute or tents need to be booked much further in advance. But I have to admit, it was an authentic German cultural experience. There is a certain part of German culture that is based on a love of Americana, represented by trucker belts and hats (or rodeo belts and hats), blue jeans, and leather biker vests, among other things (such as strangely dyed and teased 1980s hair), and our tent was their home.

I arm-wrestled with Slow Ignatio, who won handily. There was a lot of sitting and talking, and in the end, less drinking than expected. Most students had predictably pre-drunk the event, and it seemed their budgets had been nearly exhausted by the food. They wanted to go out and try the midway rides with the money they had left.

The wine fest was located in the centre of a midway or what you might call a fair. It had roller coasters, a Tilt-A-Whirl ride, and things that surely don't mix well with alcohol. These things, after you've had a good soaking in the results of a local wine harvest, are just about guaranteed to make you vomit, or at least want to vomit. What were the organizers thinking? What was our school thinking? Again, about all I can say about it is that it was an authentic experience. Go to Germany. Drink your face off. Ride a roller coaster. Rinse. Repeat.

Our tent was too boring to return to after all of those festivities, but other tents had drawn huge crowds and we went to explore their contents. With the aid of mobile phones, we all ended up in the same large tent, where a much better band and better dancing were both underway. We congregated there in a huge circle and did what international exchange students do: we stood out and made a spectacle of ourselves, dancing in a huge circle, horribly drunk.

Sometime in the wee hours of the morning, some of us were ready to drop out after feeling the effects of the combined entertainments. I don't mean me. It is almost always the girls. I had met a few girls in our crew who could drink me under the table, but even these girls wanted to go home early, mainly because the boys they were drinking under the table were starting to make life difficult.

This night, or that morning, one of our girls had gotten led outside of our large dancing circle by one of these sorts and was finding it difficult to rejoin the herd. I had noticed her missing and had been casting my gaze about the massive tent trying to spot her when I saw her a long way off, looking a little like she was being kidnapped. Really someone was just holding her by the elbow, but she gave me an exasperated and exhausted look that made me go over and take her away as if she were my long-lost, mail-order, child bride. The abductor put up no further protest.

That was enough for her for the evening. We rounded up a posse of likewise exhausted females and decided to head home only to lose most of them moments later in the portable toilet maze during a much-needed bathroom break before getting back on the streetcar. Then we made the long walk to the tram stop, hoping we would reach it before the line stopped running for the night.

Karina, a student from Latvia, was tottering all over the

place and could not make it on her own, so she carried her shoes in one hand and held my hand with the other, until we were on the train and she was back in compatriot Elina's care.

The struggle bus coming back from the much bigger Oktoberfest later in the semester nearly claimed one student.

We had a fairly large contingent of American students that term, and they were always hovering around first place in the drinking wars. For Oktoberfest, we caught an early train to Munich and planned to catch a late one back that night.

Our American friends showed up at the train at about 5:30 a.m. with shopping bags filled with liquid provisions and proceeded to play drinking games all the way there, basically pre-drinking Oktoberfest.

They were loud and obnoxious. It was insanity. Gaige, our biggest American, had a body mass index that could hold more alcohol than anybody else, and he was well and truly wasted by the time we arrived many hours later.

As at Bad Dürkheim, our school had organized a place for us to eat and drink in one of the huge tents that make up the Oktoberfest landscape. Again, it was alright. The beer came in one-litre mugs, but again there was a midway and what we clearly saw were far better and more interesting tents. So the group scattered, some going to test their luck or stomachs on the games or rides, and some trying to get into completely booked tents that people made reservations for a year in advance.

At the end of it all, we congregated back at the main train station in Munich, most of us wet and uncomfortable from sudden rain showers that had descended in the evening.

Gaige was missing. Usually some student comes at the last second for one of our trips, but this time our train pulled out of the station, and Gaige was not amongst us. We had a reservation, a group ticket, and he was missing his ride home.

The friends who had been with him did not know what had happened to him. They were a bit too inebriated to recall. Seth seemed extremely agitated, worried that something bad might have happened after having seen Gaige carousing with several even-larger Germans. Seth curled up in a ball on his seat as he tried to tell us what he could recall and just kept repeating that Gaige was "dead" and rocking himself back and forth. With friends like these, who needs eyewitnesses?

It was beer's revenge. Gaige had gotten lost during a bathroom break. For some reason, when he failed to return from that, his friends simply left the tent they were in and went on to another. And then they went back to the train. Now they had visions of Gaige being slumped over somewhere, unconscious, and probably being used as a human toilet. This was unsettling to everyone within earshot, but I guess some of them found it preferable – or at least calming – not to think that Gaige was dead.

Our trip home (and it takes hours) was filled with talk about what might have happened to him, frantic phone calls to Gaige's mobile phone, our school, and our school directors, the Oktoberfest security, the Munich police, and various hospital admissions desks, but nobody turned up any sight of a drunk American kid. Well, more precisely, none of the calls turned up our missing American kid.

It probably didn't help that Gaige had gone to Oktoberfest in full costume: tan Lederhosen, boots, and a checked pink-and-white shirt. He looked exactly like one hundred thousand other young men at that moment. Good luck finding the one we needed.

In the end, the most amazing thing happened: when some of the students finally arrived home, there was Gaige, sitting nursing his excruciating hangover in their kitchen. He had somehow booked and paid for his own way home, on a more direct train than our large group could take (we had to make connections, due to the size of our group). On his own, Gaige got a seat on a more direct route and handily beat us home. He had not thought of letting anyone know.

The struggle bus could well be more than just drunken incidents. It could be a metaphor for all that is student life: the lack, the want, the discomfort, the uncertainty of things, the cheapness of it all. It can mean little things, like moving in only to discover that you need to buy absolutely everything that you chose to leave at home in your own country, mistakenly thinking a dormitory might supply such things as pots and pans. You need everything from that to dish soap to towels. The only thing provided is bed linen, and you might not like those, either.

I had been here for months, still humming and hawing about buying pots and pans, when a flash hit me: I could boil, fry, or scramble eggs, make spaghetti, or cook soup or anything I liked in one of the souvenirs I had bought, a German police officer's training mess kit, a compact collection of cookware. I was going to use them for motorcycle camping one day and had not thought to use them now, when I truly needed them. I had completely forgotten I owned them.

There is also the knowing that you have snow boots in storage at home but need a pair here, there is drinking from plastic cups when you have perfectly good wine glasses 6,000 kilometres away, and there is buying things you need now but will never need enough to want to ship home.

And despite what people say about the benefits of higher education, the struggle bus might even be a preview of life itself and all that will soon follow for many of us. Beyond all the excitement and beauty of the adventure of temporarily being in Europe or a new country lurks the possibility of a continuing mediocre middle-class (or worse) existence for many of us. Lots of students talk about the bleak prospects they see at home in their own countries, yet they know they must return there.

We have the odd rich student. We have the odd brilliant one, too, but we have a whole herd of middle-of-the-road scholars who are, according to the schools that send them to us, the bright lights of their nation's next generation. This is worrisome. If you come from some underdeveloped or impoverished or dictatorially controlled country, I am not sure whether your chances will be better or worse with fair to middling intelligence, but it is hard to get my Western mind around. Things are hard enough where I come from, and I come from next door to the home of the American dream.

School is meant to prepare us for so much that might never actually come about. What we will still need later on is luck. With or without the piece of paper that is coming our way at the end of all this schooling, life is still a numbers game.

But for now that is all in the future. Here is now, and for now, there is a large struggle bus parked outside the door in an otherwise quiet residential neighbourhood. In that sense, the underprivileged students among us have the best chance of surviving, at least on the drinking struggle bus, because the number one deterrent to student drinking is student poverty.

Our exchange students come from all over the world, and whatever nationalities we don't currently have represented can be found at the regular student get-togethers that take place around town on various nights of the week. At these, of course, the point is to get together and talk and drink with students from other schools, but some students can't economically keep pace. This is good for their grades and their livers, but not for their social lives.

I have had our one Romanian student, Tudor, text me long after I have left a party to ask it I have any beer left in my room. He will come by to get one so that he can stay in a kitchen longer and not stand around with nothing in his hand. He is a thinker, Tudor is, a technical genius, but his hailing from Romania sometimes puts him at a disadvantage, even in comparison to myself.

But Spanish students, as a contingent, have the least money this time around. Sometimes it will be a student from some former Soviet-satellite country with a new and unpronounceable name (the country, not the student) and a valueless currency, but right now it is Spanish kids.

I spent a lot of time in the first term travelling all over Germany on cheap weekend train tickets with our Spanish contingent. We would sometimes take a Chilean along for language parity and translation (Spanish-to-Spanish) services, and the trips were wonderful and eyeopening. We would pack food. We couldn't afford to buy it underway, and it was a deal. On those tickets, you can literally get anywhere you can in 27 hours for about 8 Euros, and if it is not too far, you can sightsee and make it back all in the allowed time.

This was manna from heaven for me and the Spanish students. It left drinking budgets virtually undisturbed, and we got a better grounding in German tourist sites and geography than anyone else that term.

Being short on funds means finding solutions to problems. Spanish and Eastern Block students and myself were always finding new ways to finance ourselves. I began building and selling bicycles from scrap. Lorenzo and Tudor and I would carefully return every Pfand bottle (a bottle with a deposit on it) we could find to get the 25 cents back. They add up extremely quickly.

Another struggle for exchange students is leaving home (many people would go home to their own country for short visits due to homesickness or because they missed their mothers' cooking or their mothers never taught them one thing about living on their own).

Another is leaving boyfriends and girlfriends behind. There always seemed to be far more boys without girlfriends each semester, or at least that is how they put it. "I must find woman" does not translate directly to, "I have no girlfriend." If a girl had a boyfriend when she started on exchange, she often soon did not. Boyfriends did not appreciate their girlfriends choosing an exchange over them, and suddenly the girl would realize it might be a more interesting exchange as an available fish. Boys who had girlfriends, on the other hand, were locked in death struggles with their cell phones to try to keep the girlfriends they had on the hook until they got home.

Dorm parties, a bigger variety of kitchen party, would introduce these two sides to vast numbers of their counterparts, but there was always a horrible angst, because nobody knew who was available. People would often ask me, as if I had some insider knowledge. I barely talk about my age in this book, because I really don't feel it, but I have to admit I think people came to me to see if I knew who was single or taken because of my age.

It was kind of funny. I thought everybody would just be out there to hook up with whomever they could and not be worried about details, but that was not the case. They actually ran their choices by me to see what I thought. Some new couples did form, but none from the people who asked me for advice.

I arranged my own girlfriend for my stay in Germany, Lynne, an art- and travel-loving Australian who was teaching the children at a local castle. In that area at least, I stayed off the struggle bus.

Tankini

It seems odd to start a story not knowing how to begin it. I often start writing without knowing how things will end, but that is different. At least I know what the story is. Not knowing at all how to begin a story means I don't know exactly what the story *is*. Not knowing how it ends is a trifle in comparison.

Usually I at least know the pace, the intent, the message an event is supposed to give me (or give you) and the picture that it wants to portray. In that case, I can jump right in. But in this case, I have none of that. I only know the ending. The story leading up to it still puzzles me.

A few days spent thinking over such an event in front of a typewriter will usually work it out in my mind, and I can begin to recount it, but this event still has me baffled. Strangely, for you, this is actually good news, for stories like this can only begin in one place: at the end. Think how much time and effort you will save!

This story, then, ends in Nuremberg, in winter. Nuremberg is not that far away and makes a pleasing jaunt from my location. The city's famous Christmas market had just opened and was in full, bloated swing. If you don't already know, Nuremberg has the oldest or most famous Christmas market in Germany, or some such combination of things.

I am sorry, but to my weary shopper's eye, it is just one more big, dishevelled, outdoor junk sale full of Christmas kitsch. Sure, some of it is handmade, but a lot of it is simply an odd mix of Christmas decorations, crafts, and stores selling everything from socks to kitchenwares. It is a really strange mix of Christmas and commercial, no different than going to a Walmart where it happens to be freezing inside.

Besides that, every second stall sells either Bratwurst or alcoholic beverages, so the narrow passageways between the booths are generally even more clogged than necessary simply because some people find the market a nice place to grab a bite to eat or start to get inebriated for the coming evening. The whole town square is taken over by it, yet the market is not that big. The tourists and locals flocking to it make it burst at the seams.

Nuremberg, for all its glories (it was the birthplace and home of German artist Albrecht Dürer) was also the site of huge Nazi rallies and the later Nuremberg trials. If anything rains on the city's 1000-year-long parade, it is those two groups of events. Today, those years have oddly become a huge tourist attraction.

Busloads of curious visitors disembark daily at the newish Documentation Centre, built on the former site of those rallies. Other parts of the site were taken over by suburban housing developments years ago, before someone thought to preserve the rest of the site as a reminder to future generations.

The visitors come to see information and displays about things like the anti-Semitic Nuremberg Laws that revoked German citizenship for Jews; the local branch of a nearby concentration camp; the history of the city's extensive use of slave labour during some of those last years of that 1000-year history; and of course, they come to see the vast grounds where all of those rallies took place.

Concentration camps, as we all know, imprisoned all manner of radicals, oppositionists, religious types, thinkers, deviants, homosexuals, and other undesirables. You would think that this would be a strange site for tourists to want to visit, but it is not. The Documentation Centre is normally packed.

The Centre lies just outside the city's downtown, only two or so suburban train stops from the main railway station and that bustling (and happier) Christmas market. A quiet commuter train link takes you out there, if you don't arrive by car or tour bus.

During the week, this train probably fills up with office workers rather than tourists, but now, on the weekend, only a handful of people are riding it. The population of the wagon we are in is sparse.

Because the trip on the train is short and our group has already been wandering the streets in the cold for some time, the quick thinkers in our party trundle off to the washroom before the ride ends. We are headed for the Documentation Centre, but we are not sure exactly where it is after the train stops. Another long walk in the cold will do some of us in if we don't make a bathroom break while we have the chance.

The reason for this is that Germany is seriously challenged in its struggle to provide a working number of public washrooms, and almost all that do exist charge an entrance fee. Trains have washrooms onboard that cost nothing beyond your train fare, so it makes sense to use them before journey's end.

One of our crew headed to the front of the train to find the washroom, and after a reasonable delay, I did the same. I thought he must be on his way back by then. I walked through the mostly empty train, swaying through the successive sets of sliding glass doors dividing the cars, and finally stopped before the last one, just opposite the washroom. The washroom was still occupied, so I had a moment to look around.

And there, on the other side of that last set of glass doors, alone in the car ahead, stood a young man, probably in his late 20s or early 30s, with a decent haircut, no visible tattoos, and nothing else with him but a 10-speed bicycle, and dressed against the bitter cold of the winter day, wore nothing but (and I give this in no particular order) a hot pink pair of bicycle shorts and a matching girl's spaghetti-strapped tube top, commonly called a tankini.

Seriously.

I stopped and stared.

This was truly something different. It was bitterly cold outside. It was the dead of winter. A person would at least normally need a coat, if not an actual pair of pants. It was so cold, I thought, that the short rail journey had been a chance to warm ourselves up after the freezing Christmas market. The ride had been ideal for getting back in touch with toes nearly lost to the freezing temperatures of the day. And then I came across this incongruous scene.

The washroom was now forgotten and held none of my attention. Everything about the picture before me seemed wrong and out of place and far more interesting. The bicycle (to deal with the easier elements of the scene, for a moment), seemed an odd accoutrement, due to the lip-cracking cold of the day.

And a skinny-tired racing machine, at that? Why not a mountain bike with studded tires for the wintery roads? I like bicycling as much as the next person, and I think that in Europe, the bicycle is man's best friend. But what was this guy thinking? Was there some particular bare and frost-free path somewhere that he was headed for? How could it be anywhere near the next few frozen train stops? Was this how he spent most of his winter weekends, taking his life in his hands on his 10-speed?

If so, then it could be argued, however weakly, that the bicycle, the string top, and the shorts made some sort of sense. The colour was still unseasonal, though, as was the lightness of the fabric. A good sensible pair of grey wool hot pants and (I know, scratchy) tank top seemed to be in order for this kind of winter outing. But maybe particularly vigorous cycling made up for some of this seemingly poor choice of hosiery. I didn't know.

And the tankini top. Well, for that choice, I still, after all this time, have no words. Apparently, its only purpose was to protect his *man* nipples from the cold's frosty fingers, because it couldn't have been doing much else. It was flimsy insanity.

It also crossed my mind that perhaps he was not headed out for a ride but had already completed it and was on the return journey instead. But this thought just left me with more questions. Why would he not then have thrown on a tracksuit or some sweatpants? I just could not fathom it. He must have still been on the way to his ride. Insanity indeed!

Really, these little details were of no consequence. We have all run across convention-flouting individuals who either don't care what other people think or who themselves don't think about these things and just do them. Still, I could not stop thinking about where this young man was coming from and where on earth he could be going to.

He was so normal in every other way. He had a nice bicycle, too, the kind of racing model that costs two months' salary, and not just some piece of junk. I would consider myself lucky to have such a bicycle right now.

He had properly trimmed hair. He had a shaved face and the cyclist's shaved legs. He was certainly not homeless. He had means, perhaps an inheritance? He had probably even paid his train fare (Germans will hardly ever get on a train without paying the corresponding fare, even though they have almost universally eliminated conductors to check on this).

And you cannot be successfully homeless, clean cut, and well-shaved on a wintery morning with nothing but two flimsy pieces of womenswear and a bicycle. It is just not done. This is why homeless people lug shopping carts around with them: you need a lot of stuff to be successfully homeless. But I could not for the life of me figure out where this guy would have stuffed even a change purse to pay for his train ticket. His outfit was too sparse and too skintight.

He had some means of support, then, even if he had not brought it with him. He wasn't shivering like the rest of us. He must have just recently left some clean, well-lighted place or was headed back to one now. Somewhere there was an apartment, a house, a doting (or incredulous) mother, girlfriend, boyfriend, cat, dog, or goldfish waiting for his return, for this pink ray of sunshine to unlatch a garden gate or a front door somewhere and be home again.

He had a job or a pension or a sugar daddy or a partner or parent somewhere. Did he also have co-workers? A boss? Did they know how he spent his free time? Did he ever run across anyone he knew on these short suburban train trips, not far from the city centre? Did he do this every day? Was this his routine? Did anyone else who met him wonder about any of this? What about the salesman who sold him the bike or the person who sold him the pink ensemble?

We got off the train at the Documentation Centre, and the cyclist carried on, past the point that was once a huge rallying place for people who were bent on destroying exactly the kind of person my pink cyclist was.

After that, the rest of my time in Nuremberg seemed to pass like a slow, strange dream. I went back with Imola, a student from Hungary, to some historic corners of town because we didn't want to tour the gruesome remains of the Nationalist Socialist regime.

We opted for a bit of an art tour, but this did not exactly change the strangeness of the mood or make my trip a success. Something just seemed to be wrong with it now: the strangeness, the cold, the senseless Christmas market, the weirdness of the pink exhibitionist.

One thing that strangely wasn't being exhibited was any sort of work made by Nuremberg's star artist, Albrecht Dürer. We went to the preserved Dürer house and museum, but inside saw nothing that was original; the museum was too small and too uninfluential to have any of his pricey works. Even the furniture and tools on display were all reproductions. Everything of Dürer's had been sold after his death to provide for his widow.

As I said, maybe there is no story here, just an ending, and we should leave it at that. All I am left with is the strange contrasts. That cyclist is still out there somewhere in Nuremberg, but the city has almost nothing left of its favourite son, Dürer. That strange contrast is all I really acquired there this time around, but I will never forget either of them.

Mon Ami, Paris

What can one say or write about Paris that has not already been said or written? Lynne, who travelled with me there at Christmas (and who knew I was writing this book about my art travels) casually dropped that bomb in my lap shortly after our return, when it looked like I was itching to record what I had seen there.

And she is correct. What can still be written or said? The city, a sprawling, ancient mass of everything that man has ever deigned to fashion, design, or otherwise put on this earth, certainly suffers from overexposure in saying and writing channels. It is every writer's and artist's dream destination, and over the years it seems most of them made the dream reality by showing up at some point and creating something unforgettable in the City of Light.

Lynne's comment almost threw me into writer's block. What can one say about Paris that doesn't sound like it has been said 1,000 times? What can one write about it that has not already been written about it? A river runs through it? No, already taken. It has a Hemingway bar? Every town has a Hemingway bar, and Paris has a mixed relationship with its Hemingway bar. The one in the Ritz Hotel there was voted 'Best Bar in the World' by Forbes Magazine in 2001 but closed its door on April 16, 2012 for a planned two-year renovation. Hopefully it is open by now, but when I was there, Paris didn't even have a Hemingway bar in that sense.

Hemingway wrote *A Moveable Feast* about his Paris years, but even that title doesn't apply to everybody. Hemingway told his biographer, "If you are lucky enough to have lived in Paris as a young man, then wherever you go for the rest of your life, it stays with you, for Paris is a moveable feast."

When I first went there, I was already too old to be Hemingway's ideal candidate for drinking in the city (I mean *taking in* the city), and I couldn't stay long enough to fit his ideal either. On my first visit, I was already 33 years old and only had a few days. True, I still had my perpetual mental age of 19, but I was not studying art and missed all that. I was there for work and saw the tourist sites, and I had my girlfriend with me, one I would eventually spend a grand total of two weeks of my life with. So for a very few days, unlike the eternal Seine, I coursed through the City of Light and even missed the Eiffel Tower.

This trip would be quite similar in a way, except I would also put my back into seeing a tiny sliver of the city's endless supply of art. In that sense, Paris is simply an overwhelming buffet with an attached smorgasbord, not simply a feast. And it is hardly moveable. It is anchored to the thousand-year-old roots of the place. It is a 2,844 square kilometre maze for which I had a total of four days this time around.

Granted, on a student budget, this can seem like a long time in a moderately expensive city like Paris. Four days there costs about the same as one month of living in my student dorm, but Paris is incalculably worth the price differential. Everyone needs to one day go there, and if your goal is an art tour of Europe, then it is probably your most important port of call or close second. Even on a budget, you simply must go. Not seeing Paris due to a lack of funds is like trying to save money by making a grilled cheese sandwich without the bread. And who ever heard of a breadless sandwich?

I always seem to hit Paris in the winter, even if the Paris winter feels a bit like my spring. The air is always fantastic, the light uniquely harsh, and you always seem to be outside walking in both.

The city is too big to deal with. You have to take some small part of it to heart. For me, that is the area in the very geographical centre of the city, starting approximately at the two natural islands in the Seine (the Ile de la Cite and the neighbouring Ile Saint-Louis), then working outward through the surrounding arrondissements, which are home to most of the sites I want to see, especially the leading art museums.

Being there over Christmas holidays is both a blessing and a curse. The city can be either crowded or deserted on any particular day, and it seems fully unpredictable which it will be until you get out on the street.

We arrived Dec. 23. On Christmas Eve, we visited the Louvre with no problems of waiting in line. We took my guidebook advice and Lynne's experience of going in through a side door that to most people must resemble an entrance to an underground parking. This leads directly to an under-utilized ticket booth. If you line up at the most visible or main doors outside, you are actually only in a line to enter the building itself, not to get tickets. There is then a further line up to get into the museum exhibits.

This is important, because avoiding time wasted waiting in lines to get into the major attractions in Paris is an important part of your strategy for seeing as much of the city as possible in a reasonable amount of time. There is also a special pass you can purchase to jump the lines and join much smaller ones (still lines, unfortunately) for getting into most places, but you really need to plan on visiting a lot of attractions to make it worthwhile during a short stay. We just tried to pick the right days and times and use the kind of entrances James Bond would have a preference for.

On Christmas Day, we were able to get into Notre Dame cathedral just in time for one of the services whereas, the day before, we could not even get near its entrance due to the huge crowd formed outside. All I can think is that most people thought there would be no way to get into Notre Dame on the true holy day. Others might have felt uncomfortable about being there on such a big day, so they swarmed the place the day before. On

Christmas Day, we were able to walk around and throughout the entire building, while television crews from around the world shot footage of the Christmas services taking place.

On Boxing Day, instead of buying a big-ass TV in some French version of Le Walmart, we took in the Petit Palais museum, among others, and on the last day, I got up extremely early in the morning to walk up to the top of Montmarte and across the river to the Eiffel Tower before heading back to the hotel and then the return train home.

No matter where you go or what you look at, Paris is magical. The crowds shifting aimlessly up and down the brightly lit Champs-Elysees at night, the sun seekers going to the Jardin des Tuileries to buy enormously expensive sandwiches and sit on enormously uncomfortable park chairs.

You can say whatever you want about the relative merits of all these wonderful attractions or attributes of Paris, but in the end, there is but one ring to rule them all, and that most certainly (in Paris) has got to be the *Mona Lisa*.

This 500-year-old lady has been called the best-known, most-visited, most-written-about and copied work of art on Earth. If you have not seen or heard of this painting, you have been living under a rock that is located under another rock on a distant planet, or you have been living in a trailer park.

However, it has not always been this way for this famous lady painted on a plank of Lombardy poplar. The *Mona Lisa* was once much less revered than it is today. For example, back in the 1850s, the Mona had a supposed market value of some 90,000 French francs (assuredly a lot of money in today's terms), but certain works by Raphael, a younger, one-time rival to Mona's creator, Leonardo da Vinci, fetched upwards of 600,000 French francs at that time. This seems inconceivable to us today.

But there is more. While on display in France early on, the *Mona Lisa* was copied by aspiring and professional artists alike at about only half the rate that other leading paintings of the day were (paintings by Murillo, Correggio, Veronese, Titian, Greuze, Prud'hon, and other household names of the time that no average person now recognizes).

But in the race for first place in the popular mindset, the *Mona Lisa* eventually grabbed the brass ring and took off with it. After some world tours in the 1960s and 1970s, the old girl settled down for good in her bulletproof, temperature- and humidity-controlled cage in the Louvre and has not budged much since.

She patiently sits there for some six million visitors per year. Needless to say, that is part of the reason for the long lines outside. Equally needless to say, that whole business with Raphael and his overwhelming popularity and prices compared to Leonardo's work have all been put to bed. As far as the Louvre and the world at large are now concerned, the *Mona Lisa* is the star painting on the world stage.

You certainly don't come across a lot of other paintings residing behind bulletproof glass, now do you? The resulting hype of that kind of honour certainly adds to the sense that maybe this painting really is more valuable than a lot of others.

We can't actually tell if it might be the most expensive (as opposed to valuable), because it will likely never come up for sale again. But valuable? That is what the bulletproof glass is for. Most loved? Sure, and that is also what the bulletproof glass is for.

Many paintings that wind up in public collections such as museums are, in effect, priceless in that way, because the museums will never sell them. They can be ranked on value if not on price. Taking a painting off the market effectively sets its price at infinity plus one. No matter how much you might be willing to pony up for it, you can't have it, so the 'value' goes through the roof. Who knows if such a painting even has a real-world price anymore. Infinity plus one is hard to raise from a group of investors.

Nobody plays this game quite like Mona. Again though, it wasn't always like this for her. Once upon a time, she was a lady who could be bought.

The last time she was purchased, she went to her present owner, which is more or less the French state. From what I recall, she had purportedly been left to Da Vinci's assistant upon the artist's death. Da Vinci apparently could not part with the painting during his lifetime. Why Mona was never finally delivered to the patron who commissioned her, I don't know, but King Francis I of France, a sometime Da Vinci employer, purchased the portrait for 4000 ecus in his day. (I am sorry, but I don't know where to find the currency exchange quote for ecus to dollars or Pounds or whatever you use, so the 4000 ecus figure will have to stand alone. If a king bought it for that price, we should just assume it was a substantial amount of money.)

Before the painting went on tour in 1962, it was assessed for insurance purposes at around $100 million, something that must have sounded like a staggering number at the time. Adjusted for inflation only (and not for the whims of the art market), that figure only gives the *Mona Lisa* a potential value today of around $750 million. But we have to take the vagaries of the art market into consideration, otherwise it is easy to picture a long line of people quite willing to fight for the chance to hand over a mere three quarters of a billion dollars for such a unique and prized work.

In reality, the *Mona Lisa* can't be worth just $750 million, but we can't tell what it might truly bring on the open market. Lists of the world's most expensive paintings are regularly published, but even they can't or don't add to the conversation as to what 'priceless' paintings might really be worth. Most such lists only deal with concrete prices established by dealers, collectors, and auction houses actually buying and selling and reporting on sales of works of art. Priceless works don't get sold and therefore remain, well, unpriced.

The lists change constantly, too, but as I write this, Paul Cezanne's post-impressionist painting *The Card Players* from 1892-93 is the most expensive painting in the world, having been sold recently to the Royal Family of Qatar (I have no idea if they insist on the capital letters, but I am sure they could if they wanted to) for $250 million dollars. So the most expensive painting in the world at this moment is nowhere near the most valuable, which is pretty surely the *Mona Lisa*.

The art market is strange. It even bolsters the fame of paintings that never come to market, simply because they never come up for sale. It would seem more fair if paintings that had a much higher 'value' than the *Mona Lisa* the last time she was sold would also now be sitting behind bulletproof glass, but they are not. What does it all mean, Basil?

There is no other way to express a possible value for a priceless painting than to imagine what it might fetch in the open market. I know that this thought is anathema to museum people who hold the concept of something being 'priceless' as quite dear and cuddly, but standing in front of the *Mona Lisa* in a huge crowd of admirers on Christmas Eve could get you thinking that a particularly well-heeled one would be willing to put up the cash to put the old girl under their Christmas tree.

It stands to reason that putting a painting up for sale actually cheapens it and takes it out of the realm of 'priceless', kind of like when you drive a new car off the lot. The fact that the item is for sale means it is attainable, and the fact that it is attainable somehow makes it less desirable. At least it sets a target price that someone can likely meet, even if the price is far and away above what has ever been paid for a painting before.

If a museum had bought that Cezanne (actually, museums did: there are four other versions of it, or more exact, paintings in the series, all of them in museum collections), it would have ascended to that priceless category, wouldn't it? A collector or investor might be able to make a nice return on such a piece of art (perhaps double or triple their money in time), but a sale to a museum would have pushed the next price (or value?) astronomically higher.

But who can really tell? I think it is safe to say, however, that if the *Mona Lisa* ever came up for sale, its price and value would be in the billions of dollars. Obviously, at that point, only a billionaire or a corporation would be in a position to buy such a thing.

Changes in the economy can have a bearing on such things, but when today's billionaires have personal fortunes of $69 or $61 billion each (that is Carlos Slim and Bill Gates weighing in there), why wouldn't one of them pick up the *Mona Lisa* if it came to market? One or two billion spent on a painting is not going to make a dent in such a personal net worth.

Not everybody is comfortable with the idea that the *Mona Lisa* has no real price tag. There are thought to be several versions of the *Mona Lisa* in existence, painted by Da Vinci's own hand. Since shortly before World War I, some owners of these other versions have been trying to prove that at least one of them was done by the master himself and does have a hefty price tag, even if that price has not yet been determined.

This effort can only have one or two causes: to expose a potential masterpiece, forgotten by time, or to fix a firm price on something that has otherwise been thought to be priceless for a long, long time, and thereby make a profit from it.

The story of this particular *other* version of the *Mona Lisa* goes something like this. A little while before World War I, an English art collector named Hugh Blaker supposedly acquired a painting from a certain Somerset nobleman. The painting had been in the possession of the nobleman's family for some 100 years.

Blaker took the painting to his 'studio' (collectors more often have galleries than studios, but that is what the history says) in Isleworth, England. The painting then became known as the *Isleworth Mona Lisa*.

Much could be said about how this painting, which seems to depict a younger, fresher Lisa, differs from the Louvre's version, but for us, suffice it to say that it is not the only slightly different Lisa floating around out there. Another painting, called the *Vernon Mona Lisa*, makes a similar claim.

What really sets the *Isleworth Mona Lisa* apart is that a group of investors has formed around it to help promote and prove its provenance and then set a price tag on it, which they are clearly hoping is going to be enormous and make all their efforts worthwhile.

This is an amazing and amazingly self-serving undertaking, if you think about it, but it has deep roots in the art world.

I mean, if you were an art collector who was lucky enough to come upon a painting, in the possession of some nobleman down on his luck, who needed to sell, and that painting looked an awful lot (at least to you) like the *Mona Lisa*, and you were able (although it took generations and further changes in ownership) to get enough money and expertise together to prove that what you had was an almost exact duplicate of what might well be the world's most expensive (or valuable) painting, well then, why wouldn't you do everything you could to prove that it was?

And then, of course, cash out.

The weird thing is that most accounts swear to the fact that Da Vinci never finished a painting in his life, so it seems a bit strange that there would be so many fully functioning Mona Lisas floating around. At least we can imagine that Da Vinci was not just sitting around when he wasn't otherwise occupied inventing the helicopter.

Anyhow, back to our story. The current Isleworth people planned to unveil their version of the *Mona Lisa* for the first time on September 27, 2012, just shortly after I landed on European soil, and not far away (the painting is in Zurich).

Who knows what the outcome will be? (You can follow the story on the group's website at www.monalisa.org, but at this point, there has been no news posted since that 2012 debut. Hopefully that changes soon.)

It does seem funny that there are always experts willing to argue both sides of any such question. One group claims their version is the only real one. Another just-as-qualified group offers the opposite view. It makes you wonder how much is truth and how much is just faith. Will I someday champion some miniature as the unknown work of a master who was known in his lifetime only to have painted skyscraper-sized canvases? For my own gain? And will I firmly believe it?

It is interesting to think of what will happen to the value and reputation of the bulletproof *Mona Lisa* if another one is found to be by Leonardo, too. What if the new one is in some way finer or better than the one we now know? Will the current one get moved outside of the humidity-controlled case so that the new harpie can be hung there in her place? How will the six million people per year who visit the current Mona feel about this?

One thing is sure: if there is a second *Mona Lisa* and the Louvre ever acquires it, they had both better get a protective case. Although the current *Mona Lisa* has been damaged a few times by indignant visitors, it was most seriously endangered when it was completely stolen (and subsequently lost for two years) when a museum employee famously hid in a broom closet and then walked out with the painting under his coat after closing time.

It certainly is a lovely painting, and it certainly draws the crowds. Whereas in the rooms leading up to the *Mona Lisa*, the gallery attendants often doze in their seats or text distractedly on their mobile phones, the ones around the *Mona Lisa* are visibly alert and actively keeping order around the great painting.

The curved, wooden railing that forms a barrier in front of the painting's glass enclosure has been supplemented lately with a crowd-controlling rope. People press up as close as they can to these two obstacles, because the *Mona Lisa* is actually quite small and is doubly hard to see through the thick, green glass of its case. Visitors raise their cameras and cell phones above their heads and shoot photos which will eventually give them a better view of the portrait than they were able to glean with their own eyes.

It is kind of funny, that. All that standing around to get a photo so that you can later see the thing well enough. And all that work of going to Europe to do it. It is said that the average visitor looks at the *Mona Lisa* for a grand total of 15 seconds before moving on. I think I did about the same.

I personally was much more impressed by the Albrecht Dürer self-portrait that I had seen just a few minutes before. It was simply tucked into a corner of an ill-lit adjunct room, a kind of half-garret arrangement, right under the outer roof of that part of the museum. Nobody was guarding it, despite a bus tour full of children and their guide who had descended upon it for a time, before moving off and leaving it totally alone again.

This is the wonder of studying art where it was made, or at least where it now hangs. I am always happy to locate and view a picture I have already studied in books. The backstories are worth as much as the art, but seeing the piece when you know the story is an experience. Dürer and his self-portraits have amazing backstories. He is often noted as the first Northern European artist to sign his work, declaring himself an artist and not just a common craftsman. In that sense, he elevated himself (not simply by signing his work, but rather through his whole attitude) from anonymous workman to rock star, art god.

The Louvre owns one of three remaining self-portraits by Dürer. This one hangs in the Richelieu Wing, on the second floor, Germanic countries, 16th century, Room 8, in case you ever go looking for it. Without that information, it would be hard to find. In this case, Room 8 is a tiny room with windows that let in just a little bit less than the daily recommended dose of sunlight, and there is no other light in the room. You might want to bring along a flashlight.

The Dürer portrait is stuck up against the wall, just inside a doorway, a hard left upon entering the room. The size of it is underwhelming, much like the size of the *Mona Lisa*, but the picture is a thing of beauty, unmarred by a thick glass coating. You can get right up to it, yet it gets short shrift from the museum. The Louvre's own website does not list the date or provenance of the work (that is just bothersome) and calls it *Portrait of the Artist Holding a Thistle*. Other authorities at least put a date on it: 1491 or 1493.

Some experts say that Dürer did not paint the first self-portrait in Northern Europe, but some say he did; some point out that they mean specifically painting himself as the sole or independent subject of a painting is what makes a real self-portrait. Dürer certainly painted this one early, as alternate titles call the piece *Self-portrait at 22*.

However you slice it, Dürer acted differently, and that helps make him fascinating. This portrait, not as famous as his larger and bolder Christ-like self-portrait now in Munich, might have been a gift to his parents. It really is an amazing painting, although rather lost in the vast expanse of the Louvre.

And that is, a little bit, the way everything is in this city. It really is too big to take in. But if you have the time, you can go looking in as many dark corners as you can get to in the City of Light.

Soaking in Switzerland

Going to Switzerland has always been a favourite dream of mine. For me, the country has perennially stood as the epitome of what Europe is (or should be): a naturally beautiful place where cows wear bells and crunch grass in Alpine meadows, where train schedules are kept to a precise standard, and where the world's richest bankers, industrialists, and celebrities convene with other jet setters to plot world domination or otherwise live out their fantasy lives.

The country is so well known and has such strong connotations going for it that everyone on the planet must have a very firm notion of just what the place means to them. From fine watches to fine chocolate to fine fondu, Switzerland has the best of everything, and if they don't make it, Swiss money buys it and imports it.

Along with all of this fineness comes a price. Everything in the country costs about two and a half times whatever you are accustomed to paying. Buying a Coke in a cafe is a nearly lifetime commitment, and going out for dinner (at least on a student budget) is tantamount to signing up for your first mortgage.

With all of these dangerous, knife-edge prices being flung about, a simple thing like standing in front of a cashier can be a sweaty test of your will. As each item passes over the price scanner, you are apt to feel your throat tighten and ask yourself how much you really want that banana or whether putting a downpayment on a new sailboat might be a more sensible buy.

Everyone knows this before they go to Switzerland, but still they go. They want to see what the Swiss and the world find so fascinating about the place, so they brave the expense. We were no different. Any visit to Switzerland is knowingly taking your financial future in your hands. Still, Trista, an American student, and I allowed ourselves to be swept up into the pricey vortex to see what it was all about.

I wasn't planning on visiting Switzerland right away; it just happened. We wanted to go on a short holiday during one of our breaks from school. We all want to see more of Europe. I needed to visit museums. Wanting to save money, we signed up for a blind booking promotion with a German airline. In exchange for the advance payment of a bargain-basement fare, we would be sent to one of several cities on a list.

All of the places listed were appealing, but we chose to pay a little bit extra to eliminate a few we had either recently been to or were going to in the near future. We were quite fascinated with the idea of Barcelona or some other warm and inexpensive spot with good museums.

We noticed Zurich lurking at the end of the list and discussed how getting stuck with this expensive millstone would ruin our respective budgets for the next couple of months. Plus, Zurich was so close to home we could get there more easily and cheaply by train. Flying would force us to travel two hours in the opposite direction just to reach the airport.

Somehow we did not let this data sufficiently soak in to our minds and stuck with our decision to eliminate the other cities. We plunked our credit card information into the website and hit send, and a few seconds later, we had confirmation that we were going to Zurich.

It is funny how the attainment of a long-held dream can feel like a depressing disaster, but that only lasts for a minute, then we started planning. We determined to make the best of it.

We would visit Zurich for two days and then hop over to Lucerne for another couple of days. More than that was out of the question, but this would give us a taste of the country.

Zurich is important to my studies because it is an art capital, or at least an *art market* capital. Lucerne has the feel of the Swiss countryside with the Alps towering close in over the lake in the centre of town and mountain meadows that descend almost right to its shores.

We set about mitigating the certain financial disaster that awaited us. We signed up for a ride share to the Cologne airport, the cheapest way to get there, and another for the way back five days later. We booked a room in a private home in Zurich and in a backpackers' hostel in Lucerne. We packed the minimum amount of luggage to avoid all extra costs with the airline and set off.

The ride to Cologne was perfect. The driver showed up at the appointed time and place in a brand new, immaculately clean car, and we got along well with her right off the bat. Another passenger joined us a few minutes later, but the driver had two disquieting pieces of news.

Airport security workers were on strike, she said, and most flights out of Cologne were being cancelled or delayed. In addition, from what she and friends knew from experience, the airline's blind booking system almost always sends passengers to either Zurich or Milan, so it seemed almost a sure thing that had we eliminated Zurich, we would now be on our way to much more affordable Italy.

Again, almost like not heeding the thunder as a clear warning sign of an approaching storm, we got in the car. On the way, we talked about Swiss prices, among other things. Our two travelling companions generally agreed that Switzerland presented prices with a bite like a venomous cobra and that the entire country would be coiled just as tightly (like a watch spring), ready to attack our wallets. At that moment, none of that seemed to be the problem. First we would have to get there.

We got dropped off in Cologne, grabbed a snack at

McDonald's (travelling with an American almost assures this, although we are in the middle of Europe and could choose from any number of quaint or pretty bistros or cafes), and headed for the airport.

The place did seem oddly subdued. We received boarding cards at the check-in counter, but the employees there acknowledged that the strike could result in delays, and that we should not go through security until our flight was called. This also seemed strange, given that most airlines want passengers to pass security an hour or so before boarding, but we complied and took a seat in a sparsely populated Burger King (my American friend was hungry) where we could watch the departures board.

Since we were so early arriving at the airport, I had time to leave my companion and hurry back to the train to take a short trip to my old hometown (the place the mother of my children grew up and lived until we were married). Thanks to progress, the town was now only two S-Bahn stops and a grand total of seven minutes away. I would have plenty of time. I hopped on the next train and rode back into my past to kill the time.

The people who say that you can never go home again are both absolutely right and somehow also nearly dead wrong. The train was new; it was not like the lumbering old D-Zug commuter trains of my youth, with ever-present conductors and the look of real trains about them.

The train station in my old town was also new; it had shifted to the other side of the road, probably because they built the new station while the old one was still in service, in order to minimize the interruption. New industrial buildings have crowded nearly to the edge of town, covering former fields, so the last street with houses – the one my ex-wife grew up on – is still the last street with houses in town.

The town was always particularly lifeless. It is one of those German towns where houses and shops are built right along the sidewalk, so there are no trees, grass, front yards, or fences on the main streets, and because people both walk and park on the sidewalks, every road is tight. There are many old German towns like this.

When you leave the train station, you find yourself in the oldest part of town, in what would have once been a town square. It lost that purpose long before I ever came here. This one is carved into (it was always that way) to make room for cars (or carriages, back in the day) to turn around or drop off and pick up travellers. There is a church here with the only trees between here and our old house (there are not another dozen trees in the whole town).

Low brick and half-timbered houses lie sunk, half buried in the ground. These buildings, which successive layers of sidewalk stones and road pavement seem to have partially swallowed, are the oldest ones here. I remember being fascinated and surprised by this when I came here 30 years ago, and these buildings still make me wonder how they survived so much and how their owners put up with the fact that their buildings were slowly disappearing below street level.

It no longer seems strange to me in this town where the industrial revolution came home to roost. The bleakness of the place seems to go well with the houses having given up the struggle to even be there, let alone be show homes.

Walking through town, I saw few big changes. The stationary shop where we once bought paper and pens (who writes on paper anymore?) is now a hairdresser's. The fields beyond that last street in town are now filled with those light industrial buildings I mentioned. And that street, which was a young subdivision in the 1950s with no trees or grass strips but at least small front yards, looks unchanged. The Germans and the French at that time were fascinated with Americana, and it seems impossible that someone didn't take better note of what an American suburb looked like at the time, not that suburbia today excites that many people. But still.

Nothing ever happened on that street when I lived there and probably nothing ever will. The old house looks exactly like it had when I was 17. A new family lives there, of course, and when I walked past slowly, looking at the house, a teenage girl came out and gave me a queer look. Apparently the street doesn't get many strangers either. She crossed the road to a neighbour's house, the one on the corner where my ex-wife, as a child, had some acquaintances, daughters of the local plumber.

By the time I turned back to pass the house again, the girl was crossing the street once more to meet her mother and drive off somewhere. This time they both gave me a queer look. Although I had enough time to go over and explain what I was doing, I didn't. A new family was living in the house that raised the mother of my children. People here don't just say hello on the street. What would they care about why I was there, who my wife had been, or where we had gone? I was just someone from a past they did not know. I made my way back to the train station to try my luck at catching that flight to Zurich.

When I got there, the departures board was still a sea of delays and cancellations. The picture it painted was grim. Flight after flight was cancelled or delayed. Our flight, for some reason, kept climbing the ladder towards the top of the board with nary a glitch. No message about delay or cancellation appeared beside it. Perhaps, we thought, Zurich was too important a city to have flights there postponed or cancelled, and security was processing people, albeit slowly.

We thought maybe our luck was changing. Looking back, it is now hard to believe we were so trustingly hopeful. Why on earth did we think our flight would proceed without a hitch? But still, for now, our flight was on track.

Then, when absolutely no other flight on the departures board was still on schedule, ours suddenly stooped to their level. Our departure time was pushed back one hour. That was a setback but far from the end of the world. It was our first delay. We had been boring ourselves silly at the airport only because, of our own free will, we had arrived so early. This hour, too, would pass. When it did, our flight was finally called, and we moved through the frozen mass of people clumped in front of the one operating security entrance and into the line to have ourselves and our bags scanned.

It was all a bit surreal, because everyone around us was taking the situation calmly, whereas normally, it is well known that Germans cannot endure the stress of a two-minute wait and will anxiously be on their cell phones trying to reach the office of the Chancellor if a meeting doesn't start or a streetcar doesn't arrive on time.

We, on the other hand, were going places. We shuffled forward a few metres at a time in the single line-up. It was clearly going to take hours to scan all the people in line with the one machine that was being operated. We were making progress, but to what end? There was no way we would get on the flight in time. It was like building a house where you build the swimming pool first and then dig the hole for the basement and throw all the dirt into the swimming pool.

Sure enough, a woman soon announced something at the front of the line. We were so far away we could not hear her, but the message rippled back clearly: due to the slow speed of the security checks, we would not make the flight to Zurich and we should go back to the check-in desk and make other arrangements or get taxis and hotel vouchers and reconvene for a flight in the morning.

This was a rather bright and shiny silver lining, actually, to our so far rather pitiful story. Our 70 Euro return flights had suddenly become (apart from the waiting) a taxi ride, a dinner, a night in a posh hotel in Cologne, breakfast, and a cab ride back to the airport in the morning.

It seemed like a fair trade, seeing how we were losing the money for our first night's accommodation in

Switzerland. The overnight stay in the posh hotel would be a one-day reprieve before the country next door would knock the wind out of our financial sails.

We enjoyed unburdening ourselves for a while in our luxurious rooms, doing all the things we couldn't do in our normal student digs: soaking in hot bathtubs, wearing the plushy robes and slippers, watching television, eating in a fancy restaurant, and enjoying clean refrigerators (although they were stuffed-full of mini-bar items we could do nothing with). These were bittersweet moments, for we knew that our arranged accommodations in Switzerland would be nowhere near this level of quality.

The next morning, with the airport workers' strike in abeyance, our flight took off without a hitch. Minutes later we were in Switzerland. Minutes after that, we had already been drafted onto the losing side in a five-day grudge match of the Swiss national sport: price gouging.

The price of the train ride from the airport to the city centre train station was tantamount to officially condoned pickpocketing. The fare for the streetcar ride a few short blocks from there to our apartment was a daylight mugging. The refreshments my travelling companion needed at McDonald's in Zurich (they are everywhere) were priced by the same people who rush in to sell drinking water to the homeless after a hurricane, and so it went. But our accommodation was warm and homey, the hosts happy and gay, and the weather gorgeous for it being the end of January.

We were in Switzerland proper now, housed amongst the Swiss. This was Zurich, one of the art capitals of the world, and I had a list of museums to visit. I set out to do so, but somehow on the walk downtown got sidetracked at a hi-fi shop selling the kind of vintage stereo gear favoured by my friend Brandon back home. The owner, who was displaying a lovely Revox reel-to-reel tape deck my friend would have gladly traded a non-essential body organ for, informed me that he had just seen a much less pricey

Philips machine at a flea market down the block.

I have to say I was intrigued, not so much by the idea of buying and carrying home an oversized and heavy piece of equipment from either of these places, but by the idea of finding out what a man who was selling a tape deck for the price of a small car would consider to be a "very good price." I am a flea market veteran, and now I was wondering if the Swiss conception of flea markets was the same as in every other civilized country.

The museums would have to wait; this was a quest. In the end, my companion and I both headed over to the flea market, and I am happy to say that it held to the international standards of flea market associations the world over: things were downright cheap.

Every flea market worth its fleas offers a fascinating collection of old things. It is a real bonus if those things are directly related to the area. This market, despite offering an unusual amount of Americana, housed loads of authentic Swiss items, far better than anyone would find in the numerous souvenir shops of the city. I set out to bargain my way into a Swiss memorabilia collection.

It didn't take long. If you show a Swiss your wallet, or even which pocket you keep it in, they are more than happy to abandon customers who are merely thinking things over or otherwise still making up their minds, and jump to your assistance. That doesn't mean, however, that they are all interested in bartering; some things are sacred, and sometimes that thing is a price tag.

I was lucky and in short order accumulated an original Swiss Army flashlight from the 1950s or 60s, a Swiss bicycle license plate issued by the city of Zurich, a bath towel advertising a Swiss maker of stainless steel kitchen appliances, a German courier bag that clearly mimicked the Swiss-made bags made from recycled truck tarps, and a vintage Swiss potato ricer and French fry cutter. Most of these items cost two Swiss Francs each, a steal at a couple of dollars, and certainly far less than any self-respecting can of Coke in this city.

The splurge, with an appropriate price tag, was the sleek, hand-operated, chrome and lovely potato mincing device. The potato eater cost 20 Swiss Francs. The price seemed so high that I had left the flea market before I realized this was far less than the price of a decently outfitted pizza in these parts. I rode the streetcar back to the flea market to acquire the thing. Days later, and after seeing tons of art and scenery (and souvenir shops), acquiring the potato machine remains the highlight of my trip.

With detours completed, I made a bee-line for the museums, but I soon discovered that the world of art is not only about beauty, taste, and design. In this country, it is also about money, and not just in the private galleries and auction houses.

The first museum stop, the Kunsthaus Zurich, would provide a further dip in the pool of experiences soaking my pocketbook. Even at the reduced student rate, entry here set me back 18 Swiss Francs, or almost three times what it generally costs for admission to French and German art museums. My budget was not quite ready for this, and I felt like I was handing over both my entry price and my lunch.

The museum was showing Gaugin prints and publications, which were eyeopeners for me, but the stars of the show in this museum were the Swiss, especially Alberto Giacometti, one member of a busy artistic family. The museum has been successful at acquiring large amounts of his work, with a large chunk of it having come Alberto himself and the rest from his brother Bruno's estate.

This particular Giacometti is a pretty fascinating character. The story of great art is often told through the character of such a creator. Giacometti mainly tried all kinds of styles – Cubism, primitive art, Surrealism – and left interesting contributions behind in all of them.

Artists often do this. Van Gogh tried everything when learning, and Picasso tried everything when earning. Giacometti seems to have sincerely loved being in each phase, not just trying it on like a coat or trying to make a buck off each successive style or movement.

Giacometti's piece, *Cube* (1934), is his only abstract sculpture, but even here, his experimentation almost merges with a fear of going too far off into one slim field of the unknown and the unreal. Abstract is abstract, right? Your work does not have to have any connection with the real world, but here Giacometti makes a blob (a cube, he calls it) that very slightly resembles a human head (in the widest possible interpretation). It is hard to recognize it as a human head, but at least it is not open to endless and 'abstract' discussion. The artist scratched his own portrait into the surface of the piece, giving it a de-facto face, and then for good measure, also scratched in a drawing of the studio in which he created the piece.

His paintings *Self-portrait* (1921) and *Nude* (1923) are worth the price of admission, and are simply grand.

These New Masters, like Giacometti, have been getting our attention for the past 100 years or so, but quite a few of us first fell in love with art due to the talent and works of the Old Masters, and the Kunsthaus displays some of their stunners.

Look this one up when you can: Cornelius de Heem's 1655 *Still Life with Lobster*. The backstory goes like this: When the Northern part of the Netherlands started to generate some serious profits after southern Protestants fled there to escape religious persecution and whatnot from the Spanish king, the arts turned a certain corner.

Not only was the influence and patronage of the church waning, but artists were free to find and court new clients: the growing middle class (it was probably more of an upper class, really), and customers now dictated the themes of paintings.

These themes became all manner of things: portraits in

particular, but also landscapes (as pure decoration) and still life subjects (often sumptuous settings of food). Fancy foods were only for the rich, and the rich liked you to know that they could afford such suppers (without having to invite you for dinner), so they hung pictures of what they ate (or what they claimed to have eaten) instead.

This is where de Heem's portrait of a lobster goes to work. In a free market art economy such as this, the best man ended up winning, and artists strove always to show their own best side (basically, their raw talent and mastery over their craft). So, at this time, we see many, many similar scenes of a small table overflowing with rich and exotic (and expensive) foods.

De Heem paints it so perfectly and so real you would think his life depended on it (and it probably did: a pleased patron and a perfect painting would lead to other commissions from rich clients).

Right besides de Heem's painting are others that look as if they were painted just a day either side of his painting, but all of these have some slight flaw, since de Heem's is the only one that looks absolutely photo realistic. You can stand close or far, and examine any one particular spot in the painting, and you will not find any section that does not look photographed. The painting gives absolutely no hint that it was anything but an expensive Kodak moment.

A few other Zurich gems I had never heard of: Giovanni Segantini's paintings (1858-1899) *Girl Knitting* (1888), *Vanity* (1897), and *Alpine Meadow* (1893-94) are absolutely amazing, and stunning in their fidelity to the real world.

Sure, Zurich has one of Monet's famous (but one of a billion) *Basin Aux Nympheas Avec Iris* (from a nearly endless series of a pond in his yard, 1914-22) and one of his *Der Seerosenteich Am Abend* (1916-22), but Segantini, how did he get past the censors and not make a name for himself?

This is what is and will always remain unfair in the arts, how one person 'makes it' and another doesn't, given what looks like talent cut from the same cloth. Sometimes it must come down to the force of personality when the artist is alive, and the personal myth or mystery they weave when living or that their name conjures when they are dead.

The Kunsthaus was also showing quite a number of hugely famous, privately owned paintings, among them a few of my absolute favourites, Van Gogh's *Self-portrait with bandaged ear* from 1889, and his *Cypress and tree in flower* from the same year, both completely absorbing in their virtuosity.

I could go on. Zurich is filled with museums and galleries. It has the Centre Le Corbusier, a kind of private museum/monument to the Swiss architect at the Heidi Weber Museum, housed at Hoeschgasse 8, in the only building of his I know of in Switzerland. The Dadahaus Cabaret Voltaire, where Dada (a kind of movement of non-art) got started is at Spiegelgasse 1. And the Stiftung Sammlung E.G. Buehrle, the collection of industrialist Emil Buehrle (born in Germany but Swiss from 1936 on), still says it is one of the world's great art collections, despite having been robbed of some of its works at gunpoint in 2008. However, only 200 paintings and sculptures are on display as part of a foundation, and the four that were stolen (by Cezanne, Degas, Van Gogh, and Monet) were all later recovered.

Just wandering the streets of Zurich can also be an art tour. The Grossmunster church features stained glass windows designed by Giacometti, and the Fraumunster church has stained glass windows by Marc Chagall.

In Lucerne, our next stop, we stayed in a backpacker's hostel extremely close to the famous lion monument, a statue that was carved into the rock face of a hill to commemorate Swiss Guards who were massacred during the French Revolution, when revolutionaries stormed the Swiss soldiers protecting the Tuileries Palace in Paris.

Mark Twain, who shows up sometimes in my book, once called the statue of the lion, mortally wounded, "the most mournful and moving piece of stone in the world." It is quite a sad sight. When I visited, another sign of sadness was hanging in a nearby tree: a letter, printed on a piece of burlap, from some man to some woman he had left in an airport and now regretted.

Although Lucerne also has amazing museums, I was there on the wrong days to see them. Instead, I walked out of the town, through the city wall, and up into the surrounding Alpine meadows, which descend almost to downtown. After taking in the quite fabulous views of the mountains around, I walked back down to the lakeshore, and followed it back into town, past posh hotels and extravagant villas that make you wonder what you did wrong in this life.

That is the lasting effect of Switzerland, the price differential, no matter how much you earn. The desk clerk at my hostel (perhaps not the most reliable source) told me the Swiss probably earn twice as much as Germans. Whether right or wrong, it is hard to explain why there are so many Germans walking the streets and shopping here. Their money would go so much further at home, and the Swiss, if they took the time to go to Germany to shop, could get three or four times more for their money. So it is hard to understand what goes on here in a macroeconomic sense, but it keeps the place humming.

It hummed right through us, vibrated all the change out of our pockets, and laughed all the way to the bank.

Cologne

Cologne was the next stop after Zurich and Lucerne. Our rather early flight back from Switzerland gave us the entire day to look around the historic German city that lends its name to men's smelly water everywhere.

Cologne I know well, or knew. It was the first city I really discovered when I came to Europe for the first time when I was 17. Since that was in 1982, a few things have undoubtedly changed, but not the smelly water. Cologne has been turning it out since 1709, and the most famous brand – 4711, named after the address from which it was sold – is still in business.

When I was first here, I stayed with the high school pen pal I would later marry and have two children with. Her industrial little hometown was only a short distance away, perfect for cycling to and from, which gave me my introduction to the joys of riding through the flatlands of Europe, in this case along the Rhine.

My pen pal and I got engaged at the top of the city's massive cathedral, the Dom, which, apart from almost continuous restoration work, has not changed much in the last 800 years or more. The city as a whole, in the timeless fashion of such ancient places, has changed only a little. In my mind, it will always be the first European city that left a deep impression on me and my mountain- and prairie-fed thinking.

Cologne boasts that overly impressive cathedral, a large and growing collection of Roman ruins (they keep unearthing them during construction), and museums that showcase the rich history of Roman and German culture. I had never paid much attention to such things on my previous forays into the city, but once again, this trip is meant to be different. This trip would start to make up for some of that lost time and disregard for what Europe had to offer.

I headed for the cathedral, just for old time's sake, and then to the museums. The main museum attractions are all located within walking distance from the cathedral and the main railway station right next door. During my visit, the English artist David Hockney was holding a massive show at the Museum Ludwig, with hundreds and hundreds of naive paintings of trees and forest landscapes from around his home in England, as well as some done in the United States.

This show alone could have taken the whole day. As it was, I would end up spending all of my free time in this and one other art museum and have to forgo the Roman ruins.

As usual, Hockney was using an innovative mix of paint, technology, and photography from several different points of view to give a multi-headed, Hydra-like perspective to many of the works.

There were also tons and tons of his sketchbooks open and on display in glass cases, showing the systems, thought processes, and final choices the artists makes for some of the works. Some of these books had beautiful things in them that didn't make it onto the big walls (*Warter Trees* from page 14 of a 2008 sketchbook, and *Blossom* from pages 7 and 8 of a May 25, 2009 sketchbook, for instance).

The huge painting, *Yosemite II*, from Oct. 16, 2011, was an iPad drawing that looked like modern artist Keith Haring had fallen on a national park and was trying in vain to get up again.

A nine-screen video installation showed a country road in four seasons from nine ever-so-slightly different points of view. It was truly quite wonderful, discovering how you can just look at a road so intently, albeit from all those slightly different angles, without much happening in the frames, except that a car passes during one loop.

Hockney does the same thing in paint for three trees near Thixendale (I have no idea where that is), and they are quite wonderful, too.

IPads on walls showed how his digital drawings were made, step-by-step. Still photos of him painting pieces in the show demonstrate the same thing, both in and out of the studio. In another room, you encounter 50 huge paintings of the arrival of spring in Woldgate, East Yorkshire, in 2011, from Jan. 1 onward, sometimes with two paintings from the same day. These are so simple and beautiful, you would kill to have one of them. It is what makes Hockney an institution.

He paints in so many different styles and seems to be utterly in love with doing it. His *May Blossom on the Roman Road* (2009) looks like Vincent van Gogh painted the backgrounds for an episode of *The Flintstones*, all staccato stabs but with round and blobby elements, too. And his famous photo collages are still great. *The Desk* (from July 1, 1984, edition 18/20) was on display, and shows his desk from I don't know how many different photographs and angles; it is like looking at it through a fly's eye, but the fly is on Alice, and Alice is in Wonderland. And the simple and direct charcoal drawing, *More Crooked Timber on Woldgate* from 2008 is sublime.

On this museum visit, I felt for the first time that I was actually making progress in understanding (or at least appreciating) a broader range of art than I had in the past, despite my studies. It struck me that this might be a bit of a new beginning, whereas I had often felt that I did not understand a lot of works before.

Another show at the Ludwig that day, examining the wasteful ways of Western civilization, had some great works I might not have once appreciated. A photo by Zoe Leonard, *Orange Apples* (2001/2002), was a C-print that stood out, and three other photographs in black and white showed tormented trees trying to live in and adjust to their man-made surroundings.

An installation, *Tree* (1997/2011) featured a tree held to the wall via a metal bracket, with cables, plates, and bolts attaching about 16 pieces of bucked up tree trunk and limbs to one another, reassembling the tree, so to speak, as if to say that this is what we are doing to everything, and this is all we will have left, if we are not more careful about the future.

Eleven Ansel Adams prints from *American Places* showed a slightly less used-up landscape, but William Eggleston's *Los Alamos* photos (a portion of them) showed an American landscape only 50 years ago but already in decay.

And don't get me started on the German Expressionist paintings at the Museum Ludwig. They are so famous, you can look them up anywhere, and – if Hockney hadn't been there – would have held my attention for the entire day.

German art is kind of what you should come to a city like Cologne for. It is not the huge, international melting pot that Paris is, so I left the Englishman behind and went in search of more of it.

At the Wallraf-Richartz Museum, the art starts, as the museum says, "before art was art." It houses mostly religious paintings from medieval times, many of them done locally by names only art students or scholars would now recognize, but who were masters of their craft and sometimes fairly wealthy burghers of the city, to boot.

After all, painters at that time (and right up until we started to call anything you cared to fling at it art) had to be real masters of their craft. They couldn't just splatter paint around. Their work was a craft, a difficult and highly specialized one, that they apprenticed for years to work at and then practiced forever. It was not art, but we certainly think of it as art today.

These craftsmen did well, sometimes as well as any famous artist you can think of today. Stefan Lochner was one of these esteemed masters. He painted *The Madonna in the Rose Bower* sometime between in the working years

1440-1442 (even his life years are unclear, stated as either 1400 or 1410 to 1451). It is filled with countless details that tell a complex theological story in a tight space, painted at the top of his form and in his signature, late-Gothic, infinitely detailed style.

If you are looking for depictions of child angels, this is the place to go for them. The painting's symbolism is largely lost on viewers today but would have been implicitly understood at the time. Such is art (or craft): the maker passes on and sometimes, too, does their message. Luckily, people study this (and the Bible) and can put two and two together for us in the museum cards that hang beside each painting. That way, the painter's legacy does not get lost.

Everything else does, though. Lochner was a star in his day, whenever exactly that was. Even Albrecht Dürer, who would become the enduring rock star of German art just a generation or so later, came to Cologne for a study tour (in 1520) to see what local masters like Lochner had gotten down in paint. Dürer twice paid a tip (one time three silver pennies, and another time, two) to see a Lochner painting, *Altar of the City Patrons*, done about 1440.

Such paintings were not signed by their creators at the time, so it seems fair that Dürer paid an ever-decreasing tip to see it, because (although it was great) he had to simply believe it was by the master himself. Dürer later popularized the idea of signing one's work, in keeping with his own developing rock god personality.

It is actually through an entry in Dürer's journal that art historians were able to precisely peg the altarpiece as being Lochner's work in the first place. That is a further example of how painters get but then often lose their reputations. Time erases almost everything.

Lochner was not from Cologne. He came to the city about 1442 as a decorative painter, but he must have quickly established himself as a talented master of more important types of works, for two years later he bought two houses in the city "at considerable expense", the museum notes. He was elected to town council by the painters' guild, and things must have been going along quite nicely for him.

But just a few years later, he had financial difficulties, probably died from the plague in the same year his parents died hundreds of kilometres away in the south of Germany, and his houses were signed over to a creditor to later become the home of other local painters (Bartholomaus Bruyn the Elder, being one of them), and Lochner's self and reputation and considerable talents passed quietly out of this world.

Many of the paintings from Middle Ages Cologne show "the enormous tension that accompanied people's lives during the middle ages," says the museum. The daily reality then was one of real worries about life and death and what happens after. Eternal life or eternal damnation were the only two possibilities, people thought.

The symbolism embodied in the religious paintings of the time, still largely lost on me despite my growing knowledge, concerned those ever-present worries. The museum gave many examples of these symbols, and I made lists of them. The one I remember most without looking back is that a closed garden wall surrounding a woman meant that she was a virgin, or pure. So there you go. That might be something you would miss in a simple viewing of the picture, along with the fact that racier pictures of the time presumably featured a woman with the garden gate flung open or knocked off its hinges entirely. Get it?

Humour was not out of place at the time, or at least it looks like humour to us today. A painting called *The Arrest of Christ* by the Meister of the Karlsruh Passion (the museum thinks that might have been Hans Hirtz) from Strasbourg, painted about 1444-1445, shows what looks like a platoon of cartoon dwarves arresting Christ.

We are pretty sure that, if Christ was actually arrested,

it would not have been a band of dwarves falling all over their little selves who were dispatched to grab hold of this tall and slender human. Maybe a few dwarves were sent but not a host of them, as pictured here. But who knows if the Meister or earlier viewers thought this was funny?

Dürer also has some work that ended up in Cologne. It certainly is not medieval anymore, his *Piper & Drummer* from about 1503-1504, in which a piper pipes to cheer up Job after "a hard test", the theft of his flock. This painting is one of several in which Dürer, still working on his own public persona, paints himself into his picture, this time as the drummer. It is a snapshot of a rock star in the making.

Cologne's selection of paintings goes on and on. Part of the reason for this (but this would be true of every city) is that, in the 17th century, collecting paintings became quite the thing to do, and the rich and famous had the means and more or less safe conditions for keeping paintings. People set up their own galleries in their houses, old paintings were cared for, new ones actively sought, and connoisseurs born. No more was art craft, now it was true art.

Paintings were seen as investments and could be used as forms of payment or exchange. The collectors were not entirely wrong. The city has a Rembrandt self-portrait from 1662-1663, Henri Edmond Cross' *Sunset Near the Sea*, Paul Cezanne's *Still Life With Pears* (1895-1900), Vincent van Gogh's *Drawbridge at Arles* (1888, one of four versions he painted), and even some of those ever-present *Water Lillies* by Claude Monet (this one from about 1915). Gustave Courbet's *The Beach* (an 1865 palette painting filled with raw energy and danger) is a brooding evocation of the mastery of nature over all else.

This later batch of artists (certainly not all of them) benefitted from this ongoing love of collecting paintings. German artist Franz von Lenback, whose work is also on display in the Museum Ludwig, was one of the luckier ones. He said he lived the life of a prince from the income from his paintings for the upper class. Of course, this all ended with his death in 1904, as everything does.

My trip to Switzerland and back was also at an end, almost. Our home journey skirted all airport disasters, but the ride share we had booked did not materialize. We then had to take a train, which cost nearly as much as our flight, through the hinterlands between Cologne and Mannheim.

On some side stretch of track below Bonn, our train began slowing down and was barely operating when an announcement came over the PA system that technical difficulties were interrupting our progress. This went on until we were a total of four hours late arriving back in Mannheim, tired from the marathon journey but richer for the experience.

The Efficiency Myth

Everybody knows the Grimm Brothers and their collection of classic (but grim) German fairy tales. Those appalling but appealing stories are almost universally accepted as subliminal, tough-love guidelines for rearing good, upstanding children (and, if not, well, then intentionally losing them in dark places).

The message clearly is, if children don't do what you ask of them, you basically throw them in the next hot oven you come across. The stories are almost all the same; you feel like they were all punched out of the same cold piece of German storytelling steel. The timeless plot unfolds over and over again: bad things happen to good people even if they are only *temporarily* being bad. So you better watch out. To submit is to behave.

But also – as if there really is a Gott – miraculous things occur to save those newly chastised (and sometimes charred) individuals, *if they survive*, turning them into wiser, older people (results may vary: do not try this at home).

Sometimes the tables are turned and good people get back their own (unless there has already been a drowning, a burning, or an eating of someone), as if to say that sometimes the punishment is too strong and the transgression too small.

Just as happens every week in suburban shopping malls, in Grimm Brother stories people lose their kids. Or they end up spending the better part of their best years locked up in high towers or low dungeons on some kind of starvation diets, and without any nice things.

But eventually, even if it takes an inordinate amount of time, it all works out the way it should: the bad are punished and the good are usually very nearly (if not fully) compensated for their sufferings.

We all know and delight in these world-famous myths. Some of them might even contain a grain or two of truth or be based on actual events, and no matter how supernatural or outlandish they sometimes sound, the stories strike us as being somehow reflective of the truth. They are somehow, despite their plethora of otherworldly creatures and events, recognizable in our day-to-day lives, and the incessant retelling of the tales makes them seem even more true.

That is how a myth is created: it is told a million times to gullible people until it seems real enough to touch but so that they no longer question the dragon in the room (there is always a dragon). The presence of the dragon proves we are dealing with a myth, but we willingly overlook this in accepting the myth rather than using the presence of the dragon to expose it.

Today a far greater myth is building itself in this country, but no modern storyteller has seemed to grasp it. No chronicler has gone out amongst the people, like the Grimm Brothers did, heard the telling and the retelling of the myth, and come back and written it down in order to expose it. That is, until now. We might still have to wait a long time to find out the ending of this modern myth, because the story is still being built, but I tell you, the myth is clear.

This story, this myth of epic proportions, is the German Efficiency Myth.

What's that, you ask? Isn't Germany inherently efficient? Don't Germans live and breath for order and progress? Isn't it a kind of heresy to call German efficiency 'a sinking ship'? Well, let me tell you about all that.

For some time now (more than 100 years) Germany has been basically milking favourable reviews and a shiny world image of being highly technological and efficient. If the word efficiency popped up in a spelling bee, you would probably spend more time thinking about one or two countries like Germany than trying to spell the word. Germany comes in at position 1 or 2 on most mental lists (was your other answer Switzerland?) of efficient nations. Not many peoples are thought to be as technical, orderly, and efficient as the Germans.

I can hardly start to list the many German products and firms that trade off of this reputation for enhanced efficiency. But having been here for some time now, and having soaked in the near legal limit of Germanness, I can, in looking back, say that there has been a problem with nearly every aspect of this supposedly efficient society that I have come into contact with.

German companies, organizations, and people have been living off their dead laurels for so long now that they don't even seem to notice that German efficiency has flown the coop. The sinking ship is now on fire.

There have been countless incidents of inefficiency since my arrival. Recounting them would be a dreary task, but like the Grimm tales, not every story has a sobering ending; some work out as well as possible given the circumstances or chain of events.

I just had one of those days, and it did not all end badly. The only time that this dilapidated circus that is the current state of German inefficiency has ever benefitted me was this very evening when the combination of an ice storm and out-of-order trains worked to my advantage in the slightest of ways.

This is no heartwarming story of success but neither is it a total loss, so it is very fairy tale like. Read it, if you wish.

I had to go to a meeting in the Innenstadt (the city centre), and by the time I headed out, the day had turned grey and rainy. The problem was, it was the middle of January and just about freezing outside, as it had been for days. Rain, at this temperature, nearly always means one thing: that you will be buying new windshield wipers tomorrow after tearing off your current ones trying to loosen them from the frozen grip of ice. Rain in January means freezing rain, an ice storm.

Still, as I left home, it wasn't exactly Götterdämmerung (kind of a disastrous conclusion of events). The weather gods were not trying to knock people off their feet or indiscriminately break hips, but it was getting slippery. And it was still early. It was a light rain, but one that was beginning to stick to everything, which meant I couldn't stick to anything at all. I slipped and slid to the streetcar station and didn't know how much worse it would become.

The streetcar, to its credit, arrived almost exactly on time according to the electronic sign, normally a pretty good indicator of a journey's future prospects of success, but in this case, that would be the end of the good times.

As soon as I stepped on the train and took a seat, I sensed problems. As the train slowly moved forward, I noticed that people walking outside, although beginning to slip and slide like me, were easily able to keep up with the speed of the train and soon even surpassed our top speed. The train was, in fact, going nowhere fast. It hopped and grunted on the tracks and moved forward more slowly than the pedestrians outside. A few minutes later, with the train barely limping along, I noticed those same pedestrians doing about the same thing, no longer moving forward any faster than we were. The ice on the sidewalks was building fast, becoming thicker and more permanent, and people were now making almost no progress at all.

The most amazing thing was that I, and the train, just kept trying. There was nothing to do but sit still while the train, its electrical connection to the overhead power wires and the tracks before its wheels started to ice over and become inoperable and impassable. Soon our meagre attempts at motion were put out of their misery by a disabled train on the track in front of us. Now nothing was moving at all. I called ahead to announce that I would be late for the meeting.

There is no workaround for a train stuck on a track in front of you. When your own barely moving train comes up behind one that is not moving at all, you suddenly find yourself – transported, although it is a poor word choice here – onto an equally unmoving train. You cannot just pick the thing up and go around the obstructing train. As efficient as rail is intended to be, this is a real drawback to that system of transport.

Surprisingly, as opposed to the usual groaning and moaning you would expect to hear at that exact moment, the passengers on the train started to giggle and then laugh in unison at how comical the situation had become. I have never heard so many Germans laugh at the same thing, and not at a problem. It was disquieting.

I eventually had to slide my way to the meeting. It took place as normal. Th lights stayed on. No signs of the havoc outside were felt within.

Afterward, outside again, I found a streetcar sitting at a nearby stop, all of its doors flung open despite the cold. It was pointed in the direction I had to go, so I boarded and sat down. The lights were on but the doors never closed and the streetcar went nowhere. I must have sat on it for 10 more minutes as various people got on and off and asked each other if they knew what was happening. The driver either sat in his cab or got out to have a cigarette on the platform without coming through the car to tell us anything.

I finally decided to get off the train and again brave the slick streets after the driver poked his head inside to tell us the entire streetcar system was iced over and out of service; no trains would be running until the next day at least. All trains would remain standing where they were and be shut down, despite whether they were on top of bridges or blocking traffic or in the middle of intersections. I noticed a profound lack of giggling this time.

That in itself is funny, because the announcement was fairly helpful. Germans are not that good at giving out much useful information. You will see this if you come here. One fact delivered does not necessarily lead to the delivery of the next fact that would be crucially useful if you just had both facts delivered to you at the same time, and so on. When someone says, for instance, that the trains are not running, that is about as far as it goes. They will not usually just launch in and tell you how you *could* possibly get home with some other form of transport, even if they know. You need to ask them. How can they know that you don't know the other way? That is the assumption made here. It is a system I am not used to.

I knew that from my current location, I could walk home (under normal conditions) in about 45 minutes, but other people on the train were talking like they lived in the next town or further, and were really starting to wonder how they were going to escape Mannheim this night. There were taxis, of course (almost nothing stops taxis), and traffic had not diminished despite dangerous road conditions. I also noticed that buses were still running. Walking was by now extremely difficult, it seemed, but I careened over to the bus stop nearby, from which a bus could take me home.

The electronic sign at the stop said the bus would come in 15 minutes. Although it was below freezing, the ice rain had stopped, and it didn't seem like a bad idea to just wait for the bus and be taken almost to my door, but of course, this would prove to be too good to be true.

The bus arrived on time, another laudable performance under these conditions, I thought. Its little electric route number indicated it was the right bus, heading to the correct destination, and – freezing – I was glad to climb on board. The driver said nothing to me; he just stopped and picked me up and drove on.

The trip started fairly well, the ice on the roads seemingly less of a problem for tires than for train tracks, and the bus headed off for the next stop. But that was the end of the trip. At that stop (the first stop after I boarded and a short distance from the main railway station at the foot of town), the driver pulled over and announced that this was his last stop and that the bus – and I will translate this for you – was "going into service elsewhere."

I took a few good moments to recover from that bit of information. Elsewhere? When I asked the driver which bus would then be completing the journey homeward, he said he didn't know, maybe the next one. This particular bus stop also had no electronic sign showing the schedule. That was the icing on this frozen cake.

It was Sunday night. Buses were already on a thin rotation at this time. The ice storm could not have been helping, and it was apparent that changes were being made on the fly, probably to replace buses that had crashed or had some other kind of problem. It would be at least another 15 minutes before the next bus on this route would come by to take stranded passengers like myself any further, and there was no guarantee one would come at all or go any further than this one had, dumping its human cargo and being called into service somewhere else.

It began to look like walking would be the only way to keep my body heat high enough to not go into hypothermia, but the bus had taken me further from my destination. Not only would the walk be lengthened, it would be treacherous. The sidewalks seemed coated with personal lubricant. An efficient, technological people could not engineer a more slippery, friction-free surface. Despite all of this, I decided it was foolhardy to take my chances on the capriciousness of the next driver and so, with city lights shimmering on the frozen pavement, I headed off toward home.

I decided to take a quiet side street that did not have the baffled crowds milling around waiting at successive streetcar stations for trams that would not be coming, but the sidewalk and road (I tried both) were exceptionally slippery, due to a lack of traffic. I worked my way back to the main pedestrian thoroughfare to see if I could benefit in some way from the passing of a thousand feet. And then my luck changed a tiny bit.

In front of a busy cinema, a man stopped me. This does not happen often. I took off my headphones and heard him say he had a free ticket to the movie if I wanted it; the friend it was meant for could not make it due to the ice storm. Did I want it?

Funny, but I hesitated. Almost no German voluntarily speaks to me when I am just passing by, much less pulls me over to try out a good deed on me. I have grown unused to random acts of kindness, but I was in need of cheering up, the cinema would be warm and dry and after a few hours, perhaps the situation outside would have become better. It seemed a bit of a lucky break, although I would end up sitting right beside the man offering me the ticket. Oh well, how bad could that be? The evening couldn't get worse.

I took the ticket and went inside the theatre. The film was a mystery preview, offered to gauge audience interest in a new film. The movie was enjoyable and reminded me of home, not because it was set in Los Angeles 50 years ago, but because it featured at least one Canadian actor named Ryan. Two hours later, around 10 p.m., I was back out in the real world.

It looked like someone had now dumped coconut flakes on that personal lubricant. A light dusting of snow had settled on the city. The branches of trees, lampposts, and those all-important rail lines and electrical wires for the streetcar system looked to be encased in thick wool blankets, like mile-long caterpillar pupae. No streetcars would be running under these conditions. There was nothing to do but head home on foot.

By never lifting my feet off the ground at all and just sliding them forward, the toes of my shoes building up little beachheads of white fluff with each shift in weight until the snow broke and fell away, I was able to shuffle down the pedestrian street, over the Neckar river bridge, and through the old neighbourhood that precedes mine, roughly following the streetcar tracks. No trains were running, the abandoned ones still sitting on the tracks.

It had taken about an hour to get to the last train stop on the way home, where I would finally turn and slide the last few blocks to home. People were still waiting on the train platforms, this far from downtown, and this many hours after the onset of the ice storm. What were the doing? It made no sense at all. It was still very cold outside, late at night, and no trains were going anywhere.

Suddenly, a city bus roared into this picture, driving straight down the unoccupied streetcar tracks. It swerved wildly around the sleeping trains, pulled to a stop right at the usual train platform, picked up all the waiting people, and zoomed off with them comfortably ensconced inside.

I was flabbergasted. I realized then that the train tracks are embedded in the roadway, at the same height as the surrounding pavement, and just because (during normal operation) nobody would ever think of driving on them, that (in a crisis such as this) they made an ideal roadway for the city buses that had been called into action to pick up stranded passengers from the streetcar lines. This tactic even kept the buses out of the path of other sliding or disabled vehicles that could no longer move forward due to the slickness of the pavement.

In some backhanded way, this was true German efficiency at work. There had been no warning that I knew of, but these passengers must have known the buses were coming to the streetcar stops. Perhaps they used their mobile phones to learn of this. Perhaps they just believed hard enough in the efficiency myth, and the system worked for them. I, on the other hand, a disbeliever without a smartphone, still had two or three blocks to go on foot.

The next morning, the fine dusting of granular snow still clung to every icicle and object outdoors. The national trains were still down in Mannheim. Buses were still presumably taking their place instead of running their normal schedules into the smaller neighbourhoods (like mine), but catching one would require information and then the slipping and sliding to reach one.

I thought, this time, if I want to go somewhere, I can use technology or efficiency, to get me there, like those people did on the streetcar platform last night, when they somehow knew that bus would be coming to rescue them.

I tried the transit system website, but the page would not load: its server was being queried too much.

I stayed home.

Going To Meet My Baker

One of the best things about Europe (or at least about Germany) has traditionally been its bread. The bread here was always top quality, and there are so many kinds. There is, literally, a bread for every occasion (except, perhaps, famine).

In Germany, even the humble bun (you might call it a roll), used for everything from making sandwiches to dipping in soup, has close to a hundred varieties and a dozen different names: Rundstück, Brötchen, Schripps, Laabla, Semmel, Kipfl, Weck, Weckle, Weggli, and so on.

In reality, it is just a simple lump of white bread (usually), round, small, fits in the palm of your hand, and is no big deal. It is usually crusty, but not always, and can hold many things in its grip, from sloppy pickled herring and onions to deep layers of meat, cheese, or Nutella (but not at the same time).

I am probably oversimplifying here, but there is a Museum of Bread Culture not far from here, in Ulm, that could probably set you right on more aspects of this subject.

Now, in the perfect world, I actually prefer French bread to anything else, and you can still (in France) find a baker who will make it for you. And that is a good thing, because in Germany, you can hardly find a baker left.

Sure, just as they always have, Germans live in a bread culture. They go to their nearby bakery to buy bread. They go from early morning until evening to get bags of the stuff to accompany every meal, or they sit inside some cafe-style bake joint and devour pastries with coffee. They sit outside in front of these places, at bistro tables, under umbrellas (or heat lamps and blankets, if it is a cold season) and sample the baked goods. But, in most cases, there will not be a baker within five kilometres of the place.

To continue, you can still buy any one of the three thousand or so different kinds of breads you have been buying your whole life. You just can't buy it from a baker. Those days are gone, and so are the people.

The bread you buy now was made by a machine. The small-time, hand-working baker has been replaced in most parts of Germany by a serious and pervasive move to factory baking. No human hand touched the bread or bun you see before you. From the largest city down to nearly the smallest town, bakers have been replaced by factories.

This is nothing new to this on a global scale. Canada switched to factory baking ages ago and only now has a small number of artisan bakers making a comeback with hand-made, wood-fire-baked apricot, olive, or walnut breads. For a country that has long been on the factory baking system, this is a welcome change at home.

Unfortunately, a loaf of the stuff comes with a price tag more suitable for a small home stereo unit. Still, it is an improvement on the normal white bread our baking industry has been putting out for the past half century or more.

But for Germany, formerly the land of great bread, this move to factory baking is a cultural disaster, and it will be a long time before enough artisan bakers stick their heads up out of the wreckage to wave a handmade loaf of bread at anyone.

It is ironic. Here I had returned to the land of bread's birth (okay, I can't back that up) only to find that its bakers were dead or at least retired. German bread is now produced in super factories far from the stores. Even in the tiny town I used to visit on weekends, the local baker had closed up shop and gone into business with the former miller to open a super factory of his own to spew out Brötchen for the company's bakery counters in the surrounding towns.

And that is what we get here now: bakery counters, bread service points, baked goods providers, retailers of glutinous foodstuffs. No bakers required. You can taste the lower quality of ingredients, and you have to search all over until you find a bakery counter you can mostly stand to live with.

Justifiably, the loyalty you once felt to your local baker is gone, and people at dinner parties will often talk about where they can still go to find good, fresh bread, baked by an actual human. They will discuss how to get there, at what time bread usually sells out, and what the parking situation is like in the vicinity. Factoring in the cost of gas is now the new way to discover the end price of a loaf of bread.

The fact that there are so many bakery counters in most cities and towns – when the quality of most breads today is so unremarkable – seems to be further proof that Germans (at least many of them) no longer care about the quality of their food but rather only about its price. So Germans will still patronize bread sellers who's wares are borderline at best. The better bread sellers might be slightly more overrun with customers, but even the worst still gets his share of the business.

A few real bread lovers are still to be found in Germany, and on certain days, they convene at the farmer's markets in their town squares, where they can procure huge loaves of home-baked breads.

I think these loaves (the biggest you will see anywhere) are sized this way so that the consumer can survive until the next market day. I have never seen bread bigger.

Still, this small amount of bread baking by real people in no way makes up for the rather sudden disappearance of so many professional bakers in Germany. I know it has been a while since I have been here, but where did they all go? They couldn't have all retired at once or retrained to become graphic designers and web programmers.

It is a mystery I am intrigued by but not actively working to solve. For now, I frequent a bread counter many blocks from my home (and probably miles from its factory), because it makes not bad bread.

I do not know for certain where the bread comes from. The shop is only as deep as it is wide. There is no bakery stuck on the end of it. It is part of a chain of such shops, yet I have not seen another one. It seems a little more exclusive than the ones that have a shop on every corner.

In order to get there, I pass a dozen other factory bread shops where I could just stop off and buy bread instead. I have tried most of them, but none were as good as the one I finally found. Good ones are few and far between.

I also live in a city where there is little chance of an authentic baker still existing, at least a German one. The population here is turning Turkish, and Turkish bakeries line the streets near my place.

Ironically, they have actual white-shirted, white-capped, white-aproned men inside doing things with dough, and they are the future of German hand-made baking. They don't make the hundreds of breads German's would recognize, but they are at least supporting the tradition of actually making bread.

It is strange to think that in the near future, the only hand-made bread in this country might be largely Turkish.

There must still be some honest-to-goodness German bakers out there, especially in smaller towns, and I intend to keep my eye out for them. I hope to find one close enough to my town that I can cling to in the future, but I haven't yet.

Life Imitates Artists

I have been thinking lately, well into this year-long European exchange, that being here, studying artists and their works on their home turf, really gives you a sense of how much your life parallels theirs, even if being an artist is the furthest thing from your mind (as well it should be).

Most of their lives were horrible! They often had no money, no respect, no standing in the community. They chose the wrong women or had no women at all or could only take comfort in a string of mistresses or other professionals. They drank too much, ate too little, neglected their wives, children, and personal toilette. When they did eat, sometimes it was their own paints.

They painted, in their day, things that looked like any five-year-old could have done, but after their deaths, were celebrated as geniuses. Perhaps their greatest failing was that they didn't all live 100 years longer to become the lauded billionaires they posthumously became.

I'm betting you and I won't make the extra 100 years we probably need, either. You can have your head cryogenically frozen if you want to (I'm not going to), but in truth, both that and eternal youth are probably coming too late for us. So, as things stand, our lives probably resemble the lives of artists a lot more than we might want, or more than you probably think they do.

Who knew?

After all, artists were flesh and blood. They came from various backgrounds. Some attained money or fame in their lifetimes, but mostly, they lived, loved, and lost, largely without fanfare, and in interesting times. That is probably what you are doing.

It is interesting, when bored or daydreaming, to take a moment to reflect on how closely you resemble these often pitiful beings, or if you might have liked to live as one of them, or amongst them, or at the same time. Perhaps you would have liked to have known one of them.

Which one would it be? Which one are you most like? When you think about it, the answer might surprise you.

I would have liked to have lived in Europe in the late 1880s, as it is my favourite place and that was the time of the Impressionists (or Post-Impressionists, depending on who you listen to). At that time near the end of the century, my favourite painters were hard at work and in the prime of their lives, making some of their greatest paintings and my perennial favourites, even if people at the time largely found the work to be awful.

Those same people, if alive today, would kill to have just one of those despised canvases of the time. Even the critics should have had to live those extra 100 years, to be fair.

Chief among those favourite painters of mine is Vincent van Gogh, who breezily – once he finally got the hang of painting at all – threw together some 900 paintings (some sources say it was more like 870 paintings, 150 watercolours, and 133 letter sketches) plus more than 1000 drawings in a minuscule 10-year career.

Any way you slice it, this amounts to a lot of finished work, work that – in a completely unrelated matter – nobody wanted to buy. Out of his working years from about 1881 to 1890, the best years for Van Gogh were the last (or near last) in 1888 and 1889. During those two years or so, he turned out the most amazing paintings ever made (my opinion, only).

I would have loved to have been around to see some of that taking place. I would have been present around the time of his stay in Paris (he was Dutch and the city, a magnet for artists), the year before his flight to the south of France, where he eventually found his genius but lost his mind, some say to the hot Provencal sun. (I don't know. He always seems to be wearing a hat in his paintings or depictions of him at work.)

At that time (and here again I mean the 1880s and not just Van Gogh's thin working edge at the end of them), I could have seen Corot, Seurat, Monet, Courbet, and a host of other greats of that era, working away, mostly in France. But I would have spent the greatest part of my time chasing Van Gogh.

If I close my eyes and inject myself into the story, I like to think that I might have helped persuade him to give up on the dubious decision to part with a portion of his left ear (some say after an argument with his friend, Paul Gaugin) or the even more dubious decision to finally part with his life by shooting himself (and dying slowly and horribly from the wound some days after).

I could have been there to purchase some of his paintings (my kids would thank me) at prices which would not at all have been a financial burden. I could have thereby increased the grand total of paintings sold during his lifetime (one, *Red Vineyard At Arles*, from November 5, 1888, sold during his lifetime to fellow painter Anna Boch of Villeroy & Boch fame). But as it was, I wasn't there, and *Red Vineyard* remains his only sale during his lifetime.

Painted at 'the yellow house' in Arles from memory and imagination, it is a beautiful and moving picture that comparatively few people get to see (it resides at the Pushkin Museum in Moscow) and seems much less known than his (now more famous) other works, the ones nobody wanted to buy at the time.

Anytime you think that things are not going so well for you, take a minute to give a little thought to the trials and tribulations of our friend Vincent van Gogh.

In between painting *Red Vineyard* and selling it (it took a while), Van Gogh created many other beautiful and astounding pieces. He painted his self-portrait with the bandaged ear (1889). Don't get me wrong; this is an incredible painting. Still, you have to wonder about the life that created it.

Would it not have been better to keep himself intact (or, for that matter, *alive*) just when things were finally starting to look up? I guess he couldn't have known this. He couldn't have known he was on the verge of selling something. When he fitfully removed part of his ear and then painted his dumb self staring in a mirror, his bandaged head hinting at the carnage underneath, his exhaustion with life and himself clearly written across his face, how could he have known that, 100 years hence, this would be the world view we have of him today? It is a great picture, but what a price he paid for it. He could have much more easily painted some other poor sod who had done a similar thing in a fit of rage, and held out for a few more months, painting pretty pictures, until that first cheque rolled in.

But time had run out on Vincent, and he seemed to know it. *Red Vineyard* was shown in January and February, 1890, and sold soon after. Van Gogh died July 29, 1890, two days after receiving that self-inflicted gunshot wound. It was too late for the ear, but why did he have to deprive the world of so great a gift, even if it was one-eared at the time?

Apart from the drama of those two self-inflicted incidents, I think I could have been quite happy to stand there under that burning sun (in a hat, mind you) to see how he sketched and painted the world from which all of those later masterpieces arose, the world from which he incidentally so wished to depart.

Some people maintain that, if *Red Vineyard* ever were to be sold, it would likely be the second most expensive (or valuable, there is a difference) painting in the world, after the *Mona Lisa*. (If you read the chapter on Paris, you will know the debate. I can't figure out how it would be the second most 'expensive' painting unless the *Mona Lisa* were also sold one more time.)

Not bad for a one-hit wonder (while he was alive). It is

not even his best painting. This is kind of a fitting comparison with Leonardo da Vinci, because Da Vinci painted very little. The *Mona Lisa* and maybe his *Last Supper* fresco are some of his only works actually completed and not simply drawn or otherwise worked up as cartoons or sketches for future, never started or never completed works.

It is fairly certain neither painting will ever be sold, least of all Mona. However, *Red Vineyard* will always be unique for being the only Van Gogh painting sold during his lifetime, and it is a bit unfortunate that it is housed so far away and outside of the terrain I can cover during this year.

Why do I identify so deeply with Van Gogh? I am not Dutch. I never ate paint. I think the deepest connection is that I would like to discover some kind of latent talent in myself (a more important one than being able to spot an anagram), the kind Van Gogh looked so long for in so many professions before he finally found it in a paintbrush, and I would like to do it before it is too late.

Van Gogh turned a feeble hand to all sorts of endeavours before he found painting, and he had a pretty poor start in that field, too, but look at how it turned out? Not for him, mind you, but for us now.

He first copied every fad and trend that came along, poorly. In the beginning, he must have felt miles and miles from finding any individual voice. Eventually he absorbed the lessons of all those other artists and styles and was able to develop something uniquely his own. From then on, nothing he did seemed to hark back on anything. He set off in his own bold new direction. He went where no man had gone before.

But he didn't go there entirely alone. Before he died, he had friends and supporters, fans even, and he did not pass his entire life in obscurity as we sometimes think. He was hailed during his lifetime (but at the bitter end) by some critics and many fellow artists as some kind of genius, possibly (and I quote) "from the future" (I am not kidding). His painting, *Wheatfields With Crows*, painted in Auvers in July, 1890, has been called the beginning of Modern Art.

But I think mainly, anybody who identifies with Van Gogh or his story does so because he personifies the very definition of what we think an artist is: the tortured, misunderstood soul who is so far ahead of his time that he should really be rewarded but isn't. And then he dies.

Somehow we almost take comfort in that, knowing that sometimes it just takes a really, really long time to uncover and develop the traits or skills or talents that will someday lead to reward and recognition. So Van Gogh painted and sold what could be the world's second-most expensive/valuable painting, but he never got the full measure of recognition he deserved in his lifetime. If we ever achieve even this level of success, we should count ourselves lucky.

Like I said, he might have had, in a way, a decent enough life. I know it was certainly worth living. His canvases show that it was plainly though achingly beautiful. You can feel the radiance of the sunlight trapped within them, the frenzy and energy with which he worked. You sense the speed at which he strove to capture the scenes, arrested as if the paintings were completed in a moment, like Henri Cartier-Bresson would later do with a camera, surreptitiously snapping and instantly preserving moments for all time.

Different critics or art historians can say what they like about this work, but to me there is no hidden message or cloaked symbolism in Van Gogh's paintings. It is right there on the surface. It is the beauty of life and nature, even if it is a man-made still life or the effects of the human hand on the earth (as pictured in the agricultural activity shown in *Red Vineyard*), and the honest images of himself and the people around him who shared the same surroundings and times with him.

Like you or me, he was not always alone or isolated. He

knew women. He loved (but was rejected by) his widowed cousin when he proposed to her, and perhaps that was a good thing. He didn't call it love, but he wanted to be with Sien, the sometimes homeless, sometimes pregnant prostitute who modelled for him. He called it a mutual understanding, and it worked for them for a while.

He is also remembered in his own letters to his brother and art dealer, Theo Van Gogh, although the communication was sometimes difficult. Most of the letters he wrote survive, because Theo cared enough to save them. (Theo's letters to Vincent did not make the leap into the present. Vincent seems to have let nature take its course with his brother's letters, but he wrote and wrote and wrote.) He was clearly not disconnected, not wrapped up in his own little world. He was not disregarding everything around him.

And never forget, Van Gogh's masterpieces came from a time when he must have felt like he was going through the roughest patch of his life. We sometimes find it difficult to imagine how he kept going at all, in what were surely his darkest times, yet he saw that life was a sort of heaven on earth. We should be so lucky.

This potential connection to artists that I am imagining here is not completely unrealistic. Just think of it for a minute: with eight or so billion people on the planet, not only is there someone walking around out there who probably looks darn near exactly like you, there is a high probability that someone is walking around out there who has a remarkably similar life story to yours. There almost has to be. Perhaps not in the details but in the broad lines. In addition, their story could be removed from yours by a few years, decades, even centuries, but in some way would mirror yours with a fidelity that might shock you, almost as it to prove that there is some kind of grand scheme or divine guidance of connection or, at least, that history does repeat itself.

I was never involved with art when I was in Europe

before, so I never noticed how connected we can feel to artists. All I can say now is: thank you, Mr. Van Gogh. I think I have learned something about myself.

Return Engagement at the Apocalypse

And then suddenly it happened: whatever had been happening up until that moment stopped. Until then, I had been a carefree, European exchange student, living out a youthful dream, studying art in the art capitals of Europe, and dating Lynne from Australia. I was learning the language, seeing things, going all over the place, and the next moment I was not.

And as of this particular moment, everything has pretty much become frozen in time. I have not written a word of this book for the past two months, and my poor memory is not going to be able to fill in the resulting voids. This is not even writer's block. Writer's block is where you have no stories to tell. There are stories to tell; I just don't have the willpower to tell them. Do I have to recount every last little detail of what happens to me on this trip? That would be truer, but I am not sure I would tell it all.

It is not a mid-life crisis, either. That is what everyone will surely think it is. A mid-life crisis visits itself upon you with more pomp and circumstance, I think. You suddenly restyle your life. Your hair gets a makeover, you decide to wear only vintage or eco clothing, or only vegan leather (whatever that is). You buy a monkey. Compared to the still-life I am currently living, I imagine a real mid-life crisis to be more like the last film version of *Pearl Harbour*, with lots of explosions and body parts going missing. This is not like that. Like a true still-life, this is just sitting around like a plate of dead fruit. Not much at all is moving.

It is, therefore, not a huge problem. If this were a real problem, a real crisis, something would clearly be wrong. Something would be on fire or at least inappropriately smoking. If this is a mid-life crisis, then it is the fifth one today. No need to get out of bed for that. No, I think this is just another natural state of being that we sometimes get into, like living, loving, laughing, or learning, except this one does not start with an 'L' and just has you curled up in your bed, incapable of doing anything. Maybe it does start with 'L' but the word is lethargy, or lounging.

Lying curled up in bed all day is actually good form for certain states of being. Being lazy, for instance (which you might have noticed both also begin with the correct letter). It is the recommended way to usher in the apocalypse, for example. Like a good German would be, I am just a little bit early for the appointment, it seems. So this cannot be the actual apocalypse; this can only be a personal or mini apocalypse leading up to the real thing.

They did say that the real, actual apocalypse was coming this year, but then it didn't. Which is fine, I guess. The actual date of the real thing has historically been notoriously hard to pin down. A lot of people have missed the delivery date on that one. So many, in fact, that it now seems a fool's errand for any kind of professional or semi-professional prognosticator to stake their personal reputation on. It is a wonder that people still try to predict it at all.

But they said the big one would come this year, and then it didn't. Whatever. Fewer and fewer people seem to pay attention to such things these days anyway, so hopefully the shame of either the soothsayer who predicted it or the disappointment of the believer who waited for it was no greater than when we wait at home all day for a courier or an appliance repairman who never shows up.

In my case, I really could have used the actual apocalypse for once, so it would have been nice if it could have shown up in a timely and reliable fashion. The reason? Well, I had been letting things in my personal life slide and pile up to the point where the resulting disorganization (when the long-promised real apocalypse did not materialize to wash it all away) immediately proceeded to usher in that newer, shinier, stand-in, mini-apocalypse I am currently enjoying.

Silly, isn't it? Counting on a cataclysmic event to carry off my personal problems and loose ends like so much furniture from a beach in Thailand? It is like when a person who thinks he has cancer goes out and spends a fortune only to find out their doctor graduated at the bottom of his class all those years ago, and their real problems are a thumbprint on a scan and a massive credit card debt. Can you really blame them? They had encouragement.

Don't forget, there were quite a few forecasts of impending doom (with chance of showers) in early 2013, when our story takes place, so don't get all crazy on me for hoping. Still, I realize that nobody really knows when the actual, eventual, end-all-be-all apocalypse − the big one − is coming or what it would truly look like, so it is hard to say how it was ever going to solve any problems anyway.

But I think the proper, full-blown, God-given (if that is your thing) apocalypse is probable neither a problemsolver or a problem itself. The tiny possibility that you might make it into any kind of Day 2 of the apocalypse is the problem. And that is exactly what happens when you go through an isolated, toned-down, personal apocalypse: every day is Day 2. You survived. Congratulations.

Life just goes on afterward. Not everything gets efficiently wiped out. You eventually just have to deal with the wet cleanup in Aisle 3, even if you and Aisle 3 both got a little bit burnt along the way.

Not everything has to be your fault, either. Sometimes, just as in the big one, the mini apocalypse just settles itself upon you, and you are like the joey in the pouch of a mother kangaroo that has just stepped out onto a highway. A car might or might not come along and sweep you away. Maybe today, maybe tomorrow. Whatever happens, happens. All you can do is sit back and let it play out.

Not everything that happened to me in the last 24 hours relates directly back to something that I failed to take care of or neglected for too long. Just as in the big one, there is some collateral damage, the shrapnel, hot splinters, and other people's fire and brimstone that inadvertently rains down on you. My story involves a bit of each.

The order in which these things happened might not be the order in which they appear here. In an apocalypse, things can get confusing and a bit out of hand. So bear with me, and be thankful that I am not too dazed to tell you.

First, my ex-wife's father (my kids' German grandpa) died here in Germany yesterday, after a few year's struggle with cancer. I really didn't know him anymore at that point, not since my divorce years and years ago. But it is still shocking when someone we know dies. My ex-wife, who is German but now lives in Canada, had been over here a few times in the last years to visit with him and had just managed to make it back to Germany to see her father an hour or so before he died. She said she was able to hold his hand right up until the end.

It does seem strange to have been married to someone for 17 years and then not know her father well at the end. And it is doubly strange that I would be in the same country as her parents, casually doing nothing, while she would have to rush overseas, hoping she would be there in time, and my own participation would amount only to sending a card.

Second, there was Mike and the bank. I often have very little liquid assets on hand, but I always have something of value lazing around somewhere. It is just hard to get at and thereby keeps me from getting my hands on it too easily and converting it into cash. Actually, I view this lack of liquidity as something of an asset in itself. In this case, it helps me to complete my overall Hemingway experience in Europe (the early Hemingway of the 1910s and 1920s, let's say, the one with no money, not the later, fatter

Hemingway a couple of successful novels down, flitting around Europe with a car and driver from grand hotel to grand hotel, ordering safari gear from a completely different Abercrombie & Fitch than the one you know today). I get the cafes and the bars and the deep conversation of the earlier Hemingway, but I don't get the trout fishing and the bullfights or the Abercrombie gear of the later Hemingway.

Still, money is always in short supply, no matter how much of it you have. Money is always a problem, too, both the having and the not having of it. In order to come here for this exchange year, I had had to make certain promises to myself. One of those was to never touch the small amount of capital I had back home. The reason for that was, when I returned from this trip, better educated but even broker than before, I would not be heading back to instant employment. I did not know what the future held, and I did not want to go home to immediate poverty. I wanted to have some leeway in choosing what I would next do. If I had to head home to poverty, I wanted to take my time getting there.

I also had my house project waiting for my return. I had poured the foundation for a new house the summer I left for Europe also (I think wisely) thinking that if I had that much money on hand during this trip that I would surely spend it, then have to return home without it to a completely unstarted house. So I poured the cash into concrete and would not have to go home to the overwhelming chore of starting the house from scratch with no funds. I therefore had planned to either make money along the way (picture the usual student jobs of picking grapes in a French vineyard or serving up beer in an Irish pub pretty much anywhere in Europe) or simply go without whatever consumer items I might crave during that time. I could survive either way, thanks to the planning and the economy I planned to stick to for the year.

But this week, my personal European monetary system

collapsed. The cause, obviously, was expenditures exceeding revenues, and it was not hard to see why: I had yet to pick a grape or pour a grappa for anyone for the better part of a year. Student employment didn't seem to be in the cards for me, and at the same time, my friend Mike from Montreal needed to borrow funds from me in order to finance his business.

What is ironic is that these two pressing yet separate events, occurring at exactly the same time, conspired to make withdrawing any money I still had left in savings at home inevitable. This was a terrible thing, really, but it had its reasons. I earn virtually no interest on my savings at today's interest rates, and Mike's business can't borrow money from any regular sources, so he pays me a heap of interest to help him out. He usually only needs small amounts for very short periods anyway, so it helps me greatly by giving me large percentage returns, even if they add up to only a small amount of money. I see it as being a certain number of grapes spared picking or grappas unpoured.

But getting the money free meant I had to take it out of a locked-in investment (read: fees) and transfer it to Mike (read again: fees) and leave it with him (read: risk) for a certain amount of time while I couldn't do anything else with it (read: opportunity cost) in order to make a few hundred dollars. Then, when Mike paid me back, I would have the money sitting there and would surely use it to pay down my credit card and my property tax bills back home. It wouldn't go back in my savings. I would use it to keep myself going. On top of all that, I wouldn't have that particular chunk of cash available to lend to Mike the next time he had a deal brewing.

Despite all this, I set the wheels in motion to extract the money from the claws of my investment manager and send it to Mike. But, as icing on the cake, the bank made a glitch that dangerously delayed the whole process (Mike needs the money for such short terms that every day passing seems like a week). Banking from overseas is hard enough. In order to even get started on this transaction, I had to print, sign, scan, and email a consent form. Then the money had to be taken out of my investment and moved to my savings account, from which I could email transfer it to Mike.

But everything went pear-shaped: instead of transferring the money to my bank account, the investment company mailed a cheque to my former address in Canada, where I no longer lived. I had to ask the bank to have the investment firm void the cheque and put the money in my account as planned. Five days went to heaven as I waited for this to happen, while both Mike and I were dead broke at that point. As an added bonus, Mike's client was going through the roof waiting for him to deliver the corporate T-shirts and crap that he makes for companies to promote their names. But first Mike had to pay his supplier, have the clothes printed and delivered, then bill for them, get paid, and then get the money back to me. I was going to be broker longer than he was.

This all threw me into some kind of profound depression. I don't know why. My life actually had been going along swimmingly for many months, but this latest series of events (and I guess digging into my security blanket of funds back home) really got me down. Here I was, standing in the world's most beautiful place, and I could hardly do anything. I might as well just stay in bed.

So I stayed in bed.

Other things happened, but I can't write about them yet. Someday.

In the end, what is important is that I survived and got back on the horse, and the ungrand tour could continue.

Off To The Races

I realize that a lot of my stories are about the trials and tribulations of reaching a destination – like coming to Europe at age 48 to study for an undergraduate degree – but this is not one of them.

Those other stories are all about how reaching the destination is half the fun. This story firmly comes down on the side of how getting there at all is far more than half of what makes travel gruesome. This story declares that finally arriving is the only part worth experiencing. The rest should be stuck in a dark place until well and truly composted, it is so much crap.

Lynne and I had made a date to go and see the much-loved historic car races hosted by car nut and castle dweller, Fürst Philipp zu Hohenlohe-Langenburg, from a castle not far from Lynne's. The event, which includes a show of classic cars and motorbikes with racing pedigrees, features some amazing races and hill climbs and time trials on the winding roads surrounding the hilltop castle.

Those winding roads are really razor-thin, single-lane affairs with no dividing lines painted down their centres. They also form part of the problem of attending the show, because they are used as the raceway as well as the only way to reach the elevated position of the Langenburg castle from the valley floor. The roads are either closed completely or tightly controlled during short windows between races. Due to these limitations, the organizers bus people into the area from quite far away, and visitors have the walk up the hill to the starting line near the castle.

Lynne's friend, Polly, worked at the Langenburg castle, and between the two of them, came up with a plan for the day that would hopefully help us avoid all of that hassle of driving, parking, bussing, and walking. Lynne's prince and princess were heading to the races as well and invited us to ride along with them. They were going to use their connections to drive right up to the castle. All I had to do was make it to Lynne's place early enough in the morning to be able to leave with all of them.

In theory, this is quite simple, but in practice, it turned out to be quite difficult. A quick perusal of the train schedule to her town showed that there were only two options available for getting there: take the last train at night or the first train in the morning. I am now going to explain why both of these options were dismal.

The day before the races, I had to accompany my school group on a bus trip to Neuschwanstein castle in Bavaria. This is an enduring favourite of tourists, a castle that never really was a castle at all, but was built as a kind of elaborate theatre set and hermit's headquarters for a stark-raving mad Bavarian king. It is pretty and somehow worth seeing, but we would be taking a bus early in the morning and coming back late at night, which would not fit well with getting to the castle I really needed to go to.

The trip to Neuschwanstein proved to be one of those mini travel nightmares in itself and was, prophetically, a perfect stage setting for the day that would follow. To make it short, the bus was meant to leave at 7 a.m., and as a student helper, I needed to be at it before then. To do that, I planned to ride my bicycle with Tudor and Jose to avoid getting up even earlier and waiting to catch one of the infrequent streetcars at that time of day.

When I went downstairs that morning, I found that my bicycle had once again been the victim of the bicycle locker storage wars. That means someone had taken my bicycle off of its usual storage rack spot and thrown it on the pile of broken bicycles slowly building in the corner. They had then refilled the newly available bike rack space with their own bicycle.

Who does that? Don't they know I can clearly see their bicycle parked in what was my space? And why was it always a different bicycle that was parked in my space each time this happened? Maybe they think that my bicycle is broken and un-utilized and toss it on the pile of parts as if they are doing us all a favour.

Each time it happens, I take the offending bike down, put it on the pile of broken bikes, and replace my bike in its usual space. This time, it looked like whoever was trying to send me a message sent it via the cosa nostra: my front tire had been flattened. This upset me to no end, because Tudor had my bicycle pump, and I would need it to find the hole in the tube. If I dallied, there would be neither time to fix the tire nor catch one of the few streetcars.

I decided to persevere with the bike, met Tudor and Jose, got my pump, inflated the tire, and it held air. Now I wondered if it just had a slow leak and I had been wrong about the vendetta. So we rode off in a group, but a few hundred metres later, the tire was once again flat. Now there was no going back. We were making a straight line for a streetcar station which was on our direct path to the charter bus, so I rode the bike until the rubber came right off the rim and I was on wobbly metal. Then, I hopped off and locked the bike on the next fastening I could find, told Tudor and Jose to go on without me, and ran to the streetcar two blocks away.

Reading the schedule there, I quickly realized no train was coming soon enough to get me to the bus on time. I ran across the bridge to the taxi stand that marks the beginning of downtown and got a cab to take me to the station. I arrived in plenty of time and felt quite good about how things had turned out so far.

At the bus station, some students were waiting, but none of the other student leaders were there, and there was no bus. The 7 a.m. departure time came and went, and nothing changed. Technically, at that moment, my taxi fare had been wasted: I could have waited for that streetcar that wasn't coming early enough and still been here before most students, the other student leaders, or indeed the bus itself. I could have torn off and patched and replaced my tire in the same amount of time.

Eventually a bus and driver appeared (they had been parked some distance away the entire time, rather than in the spot where we were expecting them) and most of the students had arrived. The last stragglers managed to show up 45 minutes late (who waits that long for anybody?). In that time I could have fixed my tire and stopped off to pick up a coffee and newspaper, to boot.

We then spent half the day driving to Neuschwanstein, a good 40 minutes or so walking up the road to it from the town below, another half hour or so waiting in the courtyard for our number to be called, and then were herded through it in under half an hour on the shortest guided tour ever recorded.

The place is a tourist trap, one of the worst I have ever been in. When I was first there in the 1980s, there was no reservation system, no waiting in the courtyard to enter, and no guided tour (or not a mandatory one, anyway), or my memory is totally faulty.

After our quick run through in the castle, we spent another hour getting out of it. After the tour come three consecutive gift shops in the bowels of the building, which you pass (fittingly) on your way out. Oddly, everything in the last gift shop you reach has been marked down, which means you might have overpaid if you were hasty and bought identical merchandise (for it is all identical) in the first gift shop, not knowing that two more were on their way, and that the last one is the equivalent of Woolworth's.

The latter part of the day was spent heading home (don't ask about the 40-minute dinner stop that turned into an hour and a half of, "Well, where in hell are the rest of them?" as we again waited for missing students and student leaders).

Two other things were bothersome about the

homeward leg of this particular bus tour. One was that the bus passed right by the place where I needed to be that night or the next morning in order to catch that ride in the princemobile to the car races. The second was that there is no good way to leave a bus tour you are partly in charge of organizing, even if everyone else on it is completely asleep. And so, as I have done on several occasions, I travelled right past the place where I next had to be and continued on for another hour or two toward home.

Upon arrival, I still had those two choices from earlier: either take the last train now, or the first train in the morning. Now we have reached the point where I explain why those were both terrible choices, not forgetting that one of them had to be chosen so that I could catch that promised ride.

No matter in which country you travel, there are small items of scheduling that will drive you crazy. In my case, the last train of the night had these problems: the first leg of that journey would land me in Heilbronn, a city quite a distance short of castle #1. If the train were delayed in any way whatsoever, I would miss the only connecting train that night to the next town, a town that was near enough to castle #1 to take a cab from.

Trains are so often late here, I couldn't see this coming off without a hitch, or I didn't trust that it could, but the early morning option was even worse. In order to get to the castle on time in that scenario, I would have had to get up at 4 a.m. to get on the 5:35 a.m. train, switch trains at Heidelberg minutes later for a slow commuter train to the half-deserted switching station at Bietigheim-Bissingen where I would catch a third train to Heilbronn and then a final train to (again) a town close enough from which to grab a cab to castle #1.

One other thing which is of little consequence but nevertheless true is that, both late at night and early in the morning, there is no train to the actual town in which castle #1 finds itself, but at every other part of the day, there is. So the taxis I am mentioning here are, again, only needed due to the same sort of emergency as I had experienced with my bicycle that morning.

Despite previous examples of taking multi-train trips (where I had to be on time) that all turned out to be unmitigated disasters (where I was not ultimately on time), I chose to take the morning train, because at least if I was stranded somewhere along the line, another train would eventually come, unlike the night train where the last train remains the last train for a good four to six hours, depending on where you are going, as the railroad system sleeps.

The first leg of the journey went off without a hitch. It seems that nobody can screw up a 15-minute, direct shot to the next town. The first problem appeared in Heidelberg where the next train was not waiting on its appointed track. An announcement, delivered in the indistinguishable jibberish preferred by public address systems everywhere, directed passengers to an adjacent track, but this train did not leave until eight minutes after its appointed time.

I could clearly see that this would cause me (if they made up no time during the trip) to miss the all-important connection to train #3 in the ghost town I mentioned above, which would then have the ripple effect on the fourth and final train, and then the cab ride, basically making me late for my comfy car ride in the prince's SUV right up to the gates of castle #2 for the car races.

Sure enough, the train made up no time whatsoever and deposited me in the wasteland, post-industrial, steampunk train station that is Bietigheim-Bissingen three minutes after my connecting train had departed. Three whole minutes.

It turned out that none of this really mattered. (We will get to that later.)

I spent an hour waiting for another train, eventually rolled into Heilbronn, caught a replacement train #4 after another suitable wait, and, even though trains were running to castle #1 by this late hour, chose not to wait for one and still took a cab to keep my arrival somewhat fittingly late.

I had no idea if Lynne would still be there, or had already left.

But she was still home because… Have you guessed?

The prince and princess were not going to the races, it turned out. A change of plans. Who knows what.

They said that Lynne should take the car the household staff used occasionally, and so that became the plan. We would drive, park, and then still have to take the shuttle bus up to the staging area and then walk up the mountain to the castle. Exactly as we would have had I done nothing to try to reach her castle early that morning…

All the rushing and worry and the taxi cab again had been unnecessary (taxi cabs are almost always unnecessary, it seems). We decided to calm down and have breakfast then go out and get the car and leave.

But the car was not there. Perhaps it had already left? Somehow? With some other castle staff in it? Who knew. It was not where the prince and princess thought it should be. A quick phone call to the princess revealed the car had been taken for it annual inspection. So now, there was no transport to the races.

Polly, at the other castle, had a friend who would be passing close to our castle on his way to the races, and that is how we eventually got there. This trip still included the driving, parking, bussing, and walking in both directions, but it came off without a hitch.

The castle at Langenburg, where the races were staged, occupies a great hilltop location at the edge of a quaint little town with picturesque views from most corners of it out over the steeply plummeting valley below and the rolling hills beyond. But the racing cars and motorcycles and sidecars on the streets today were the real eye-candy. And this is not just a weekend thing in Langenburg. Right outside the gates of the castle sits the Deutsche Auto

Museum, one of this castle's prince's many automobile interests.

This year was the 50th anniversary of the introduction of the iconic Porsche 911 sports car design, so the museum and the day featured a heavy slant toward Porsche racing and rally cars of all stripes, including ex-racing driver Jürgen Barth piloting his father Edgar's old (but absolutely fabulous) Porsche 718 factory team car. Edgar was a race driver, and son Jürgen, now also a fairly old man at the wheel of a car that will somehow be perpetually young, won the 1977 '24 Hours of Lemans' race (with equally famous co-drivers).

Wandering around the site with Polly was very helpful, first of all because her house was directly inside the castle gate, so we could start the afternoon off with refreshments. Then we stepped outside right into the action, took a private tour of the prince's garage (chokingly full of the last fumes of exhaust and baking engine paint wafting off the freshly driven classic cars someone had just stabled), and visited the auto museum where Polly's friends were handing out glasses of sparkling wine.

Polly pointed out the prince at the wheel of an open-top roadster, and we met the princess, watched a boatload of auto racing, and somehow happily walked down the hill at the end, took the shuttle bus once more to our distant automobile, and made our way home.

But the day was fabulous, and I would say that we definitely had half the fun.

Minor Calamities

My trip to Europe and my living in Germany do not amount to all study and play. I also have to work to support myself to make this all happen. My job at the university's International Office accomplishes this end by paying my way, but it also adds a lot to my workload. Sometimes it chops up what would otherwise be perfect travel times between classes. However, without the grand total of two hours a day I put in there, none of this would be possible.

My job here is to assist three other student helpers communicate with and manage the lives of our 40 to 50 international exchange students who come from all over the world to study with us each semester. This work can take many forms, but lately it has settled into being a type of babysitting service with aspects of emergency response work thrown in. This all came about as the result of a series of minor calamities.

It all started around Fasching. In this state (Baden-Württemberg), Fasching is local speak for carnival, a time that covers the six weeks between Ash Wednesday and Easter. It starts a bit before that, though, in good German fashion, probably because it prominently features beer.

It is a time to remember the 40-day fast of Jesus Christ (slightly less noticcable than the emphasis on beer) and provides a nice lead up to Easter, although any serious religious connotation winds up drowned in a river of beer (the streets end awash in empty bottles after carnival). Largely said to be a Catholic tradition in a largely Protestant land, the practice of whooping it up around this time of year goes back to before the time of any church and helps prove the old adage that nobody parties like a pagan.

Carnival today, if it ever was that Catholic, is now more of a drunken street fest, straight out of a pagan's worst nightmare, especially one in which he has to get up the next morning and trudge his way to the office. It is celebrated in different ways in different locations. I have seen it before, but this time I experienced it twice: in my home location of Mannheim and in Mainz (known as the party capital of Fasching), slightly to the north.

In both cities, carnival is alive and well on its way to liver disease. The celebrations also feature political commentary in the form of satirical parade floats that poke a finger in the eye of the government and ruling classes. I don't know if they accomplish much, but along with the colourful costumes and marching bands and endless procession of floats come massive hangovers and lost productivity in the following days that must, at least temporarily, thwart the plans and progress of those governments and ruling classes.

Just as they do in New Orleans or Rio and even Switzerland, people here tell themselves that they enjoy the reckless freedom of carnival. Here, it is the midwinter celebration of the coming spring. Inwardly, I'm sure people believe carnival to be a grand old time, with copious amounts of alcohol standing at the ready to reinforce the myth, but outwardly, any expression of pure and unbridled joy amongst the participants is surprisingly hard to find.

That is because carnival doesn't really change people. A dour, middle-aged insurance salesman or banker is still a dour office worker, even when dressed as a circus clown. Even if you do catch him laughing uproariously one moment, the next he is vomiting all over his own floppy shoes, and the teardrop painted in the corner of his eye seems more real than intended.

Sure, twenty-something young men lurching through the crowds, locked arm-in-arm with a group of friends, all of them already well past drunk despite the early afternoon setting, dressed like matching Smurfs, probably seems like a good time. After all, there is no documented proof that there is an end to the number of young women who are likewise roaming the streets, completely blotto, in their own matching Smurfette outfits. Clearly, this is a dating tactic that could bear fruit if these two groups should come together. And they do (there are more babies born an appropriate amount of time after carnival than at any other time of year, locals tell me).

None of this negates the fact that the rest of us have to stand by and watch these roller-derby Smurfs unintentionally but carelessly knocking over old ladies who are just trying to get their party on. None of this makes us feel better about seeing a middle-aged Pikachu urinating against the side of an office building where presumably the next morning a reduced but dedicated number of the assembled costumed characters will report for work in their civilian clothes.

This other face of carnival is far removed from any sign of its supposed roots in Jesus Christ. This face of carnival is populated by boozing children's storybook, video game, and television figures carousing through the streets. It is the sight of a lonely blue Cookie Monster pacing a solitary line, smoking a cigarette, lost in thought, alone in a sea of people, perhaps waiting for friends to show up. It is a large, fuzzy, brown bear that has entered a portable toilet and is now attempting to force its way violently backwards out of the thing but has become trapped within the confines of its plastic prison. The costume is bigger than the doorway. It went in fine, but now it is not coming back out. You just know that the bookkeeper inside is having the time of his life.

All this means carnival is probably both a little bit good and bad. Our group experienced a bit of both while visiting on Sunday, which for me was the start of a day that would feature at least five troublesome incidents which bled the fun-loving carnival spirit right out of me. There is no better way to explain the trajectory of the day than to lean on our old friend, chronological order.

The day had been going fairly well until late afternoon, when I had to take Lynne on a city bus back to the main train station, so she could travel home. We bought a bus ticket and got on a bus headed downtown with her luggage.

Part way to the train station, the bus driver simply pulled over and announced that everyone had to get off the bus. He was not going any further, he said, at least not with passengers, as the carnival parade was blocking part of his usual route.

This struck us immediately as being yet another problematic example of efficiency going downhill. Not only did nobody mention this when we got on and paid our money, nobody now had any information as to how we could continue our journey to the train station from this remote spot.

You would think that the bus driver or his planners would have known that at this exact moment on this exact day, this annual event (which requires planning) would be slicing through his route at this very moment at this very spot, and that something could have been done about it.

This annual happening has been going on presumably for the last few hundred years and for at least a few hundred years longer than there has been local bus service. You would think it would be easy enough to prepare for.

In the end, it wasn't as horrible as it was inconvenient. The luggage was alright, although heavy, and we were fit enough. It was much worse for the older lady, also burdened with an optically slimming but overweight suitcase, who disembarked with us and was a little bewildered as to how she should continue from this unexpected spot. She needed a cab, and, in another blow to efficiency in general, it occurred to all of us that there should have been at least a few taxicabs following the trail of our doomed bus, waiting like sharks to scoop people up off a sinking cruise ship, knowing the route would be blocked.

We decided to make the best of it and follow the parade towards the train station. Things started to turn in our favour, as every passing float, manned by enthusiastic revellers, threw large amounts of candies and souvenirs at the crowds. We snapped pictures and scooped up candy and made our way through the masses towards the train station. We were sometimes pelted with candies thrown with gusto but eventually turned and were out of range of even the strongest arm or heaviest candy bar.

We said our goodbyes at the train, and I headed back uptown and into the fray. I spotted part of our student group moving towards the carnival melee. Being social animals, we wanted to get together and behold this spectacle of Germans celebrating, so I joined Annegret (another student helper) and headed into the carnival madness.

We all walked together into the swarming, costumed crowd, and, as often happens, soon got split into smaller groups. We continued on that way, along one of the busiest thoroughfares in town, now completely given over to the open-air party.

Back together sometime later, Jose, a new student from Chile, had just started to ask me why Germans didn't like scarves when what I can only describe as a drunk Franciscan friar (or monk?) lunged out of the crowd and shot between us, trying to land a punch on Jose but striking his shoulder before immediately fleeing into the crowd.

This all happened in an instant. One minute we were about to discuss the intricacies of men's neckwear and the next we had been rudely interrupted and partially assaulted by a drunken member of a religious order.

It all seemed inordinately and almost lightning quick, especially given the extra large size of the monk (or friar?). The shock of it blurred events, and any memory of the scene became rapidly unclear to me.

Given more time, I could probably at least have said whether we had been attacked by a member of the Franciscan order, or whether it had indeed been a Cistercian brother or a Jesuit or something else. Moments later, in a mild state of shock, I was convincing myself that the perpetrator had been a large green Luigi character also seen fleeing the spot.

What happened for sure in this otherwise deformed dreamscape was that some friend of the costumed monk, wearing a shiny black Afro wig about four feet in diameter, stood up in front of our group and gave us some jive talk about wearing out-of-town soccer team scarves in public.

Ah ha! Now we had full disclosure. Jose was wearing a scarf from an opposing soccer club, and when our groups had been separated, had already been confronted by the monk about it. Jose was bewildered but had tucked the scarf inside his coat. Now some tiny bit of it was still showing, and the monk had once again spotted it in the crowd and tried to attack its owner once more.

We were incensed. I think the jive-talking disco escapee came within an inch of his life at that moment. I was surprised at how fast rage welled up inside us. The feeling was oddly out of place at a sort of comedy festival. I like to think of myself as a generally nonviolent person, but I think only Jose's willingness to walk away brought any of us back from the edge of a potential, disco-tinged bloodletting. The six or eight of us against this one Afro-wigged comrade left over after the departure of the padre would have surely attracted others, and violence begets violence, and so on.

Walking uptown once again, we flagged down a passing police cruiser to report the incident to the officers inside but felt they were simply adding it to the list of lawbreaking clergy, cartoon characters, and Captain Jack Sparrows already being sought, so we carried on, but the mood was broken.

No longer did I see any redeeming qualities in the

hordes of co-ed Smurfs and Smurfettes slowly but surely making their way towards each other. No more did I liken the earlier candy pelting to manna from heaven. No, now I felt only a sad, shared solitude with that smoking Cookie Monster and the shame of that obese brown bear that would eventually need help prying itself loose from the cold, lifeless grasp of that portable toilet. The group carried on, but I ditched and cut out for home.

This move turned out to be a blessing and a curse. First of all, our Chilean twins, from our batch of new students (you'll meet them later), told me they were having a flood in their bathroom. I went down to see it, and sure enough, there was so much standing water on the floor that a person could not wade into the room without rubber boots on. Even if you could make your way in there, it didn't seem very hygienic to have a bathroom that five people shared completely out of order. No water was leaking, but the showers were overflowing and not draining properly.

I called the emergency plumber. We have an emergency number to call in case of power failures or floods. The person who answered, presumably the plumber or at least some kind of employee or contractor of the student-run organization that operates our housing, seemed in no way interested in our problem. Apparently, the level of dedication, effort, and service found in the typical German Hausmeister extends its evil roots all the way down to the sub-trades.

Why this man had been assigned to answer the emergency line for floods was beyond me. He was completely disinterested in the actual flooding. He was much more interested in knowing if I had tried to do anything about it. This was a shocking line of inquiry, to my mind. I was still a little in shock from the earlier assault over the soccer scarf, but my telephone friend quickly trumped all this with another question: if I lived on the third floor, how did I come to be reporting a flood in the bathroom on the first floor? Should I not be using my own bathroom?

This may not seem like such a big deal to you, but this is pretty standard, as far as asking Germans questions goes. I don't know if I can diagram a sample conversation to show you this, but I will try:

Person 1: Question.

Person 2: Why ask me that question? Tangential answer. Question.

Person 1: Registers shock at uselessness of answer and wonders why Person 2 asks question of their own. Restates original question, possibly in a new way, to aid understanding by Person 2.

Person 2: Loses mind. Displays outrage at being asked question in childlike terms. Asks tangential question.

Person 1: Spends all his time tangentially answering second question, forgets to ask original question.

Person 2: Talks about Person 1's answer to tangential question as proof that Person 1 is not worth giving answers to.

If you ask on the street for directions to some particular spot, the most likely answer you will receive is, "Do I look like a tourist information booth?" That's pretty much how it goes.

This was all leading to the loss of a few things: my patience, my time, and my credit on my German cell phone. I told this Sherlock Holmes-cum-emergency-plumber that not only did I study at the school and live in the building but that I also worked for the school with our exchange students and therefore had knowledge of their complaints and problems and that he should come over and take care of this flood. He asked for my room number and said he would come by.

A short time later, there was a loud knocking at my door, and I opened it to the slightly red, disgruntled face of the emergency plumber. My former phone friend proceeded to tell me that the flood was in no way big enough to call him for early on a Sunday evening (as if there is some well-known better time to plan a flood). He barked that people had better things to do than waste their time fixing little things like this, but he was not specific as to what the better things were.

I realize that, at about that time on Sunday evenings, Germans are just sitting down to watch the popular crime show, *Tatort*, but crime shows play on German television at all hours of the day. I didn't see the problem if he missed a bit of this one.

After the affront of the drunken monk, I was still ready to go off like a firecracker. I was strangely primed to receive just such a visit at just such an hour from just such a person. And after living for five months in a country where that's pretty much how most basic conversations go, even if entirely unprovoked, I was prepared for this little emergency plumber. Living here keeps your argumentative skills sharp.

I immediately raised my voice. This is always a useful tactic. Mr. Plumber asked me if that is what I do where I come from: call the plumber for what he called "a little shit." I said well, yes, that is exactly who we call for "a little shit," especially if it won't go down the drain. We generally call an emergency plumber for what we call plumbing emergencies. We do not generally call an electrician for that. We don't like mixing electricity and water. And we do not discriminate against giving our full attention to a flood based simply on the size of the flood or its tendency to appear on a Sunday.

I questioned him as to whether he was just the person who answers the hotline and inspects the problems or whether he was the actual plumber. I praised him for coming to look at the problem, but said we needed someone who could actually do something about it, and that I would phone the hotline again if he was not that person.

This made him suck in air, turn on his heel, and storm off, still kicking and screaming. For some reason, I followed him to see if he actually was the plumber and was going to do something about the problem. He thankfully set to work in the middle of the bathroom exploring the central drain like an anger management escapee, sloshing around in rubber boots, and I left him to his work and headed back to my room.

I didn't make it there before calamity struck once again. Illyan, a Spanish-speaking student of Bulgarian extraction, found me in the hallway and said another student, Sefo from Turkey, had just cut his hand quite badly while opening a tin of food and that he had already lost quite a lot of blood. It had apparently, at times, been shooting clear out of his body.

That sounded bad, and we hurried back to their kitchen. I found Sefo slumped over the sink, applying pressure to his wound. I told him to keep it up and went to phone in my second emergency of the night and find a first aid kit.

I thought I had seen a first aid kit mounted on a wall somewhere in our building. Now I just had to remember where. With my mild state of shock continuing unabated from monk to plumber to blood bath, this was no easy task.

I decided to ask a long-term resident of the dorm who lived down the hall from me. I had only lived there a few months, and I thought he might point me to a first aid kit a little more quickly than I could myself. That turned out to be wrong: he did not recall ever having seen such a thing in the building in his entire time there.

I went downstairs, because I felt I'd seen a kit mounted on the wall outside the Hausmeister's office, but this turned out to be wrong. What in my memory resembled a first aid kit was in fact only the Hausmeister's usual mailbox, a big, white metal affair that looked for all the world like a first aid kit but which clearly lacked the large red or green cross typical of the species.

Then I realized why I had felt so strongly that this was where I had seen a first aid kit. There was one here, but not out here in the hallway: the first aid kit I had seen was kept inside the Hausmeister's office.

The Hausmeister was only present from 9 to 5 most days, if he could even be found. This was obviously not going well. Subconsciously, I had been thinking we could patch Sefo up and get him to a hospital clinic in a taxi, but this was wrong. We had no way to patch him up, and he was feeling too weak to get in a cab, even if one of us went with him. We thought there might be further trouble if an enraged driver found Sefo bleeding all over his cab.

We decided to call an ambulance. We are all heavily insured, but I thought (later) that Sefo's insurance would probably have wanted us to call them first to approve. But we had no time or brain cells for that. (The people who write the small print on travel insurance policies probably never had to handle a significant loss of blood while somebody else wandered around looking for the first aid kit that was locked inside a closed office.)

The medics arrived and concurred that Sefo was heading to the hospital to receive stitches, and I sent him and Illyan off together. The drivers said Sefo would be released later that night, so Illyan was needed to help get him home safely. They both had been thoroughly put off their dinner anyway, so they were the perfect match to go on this trip.

The medics perused Sefo's insurance papers (official looking, but all in Turkish), shrugged, and hauled him off to hospital. I found it a little astonishing, in this town, that one of them wasn't at least part Turkish.

Sefo and Illyan eventually returned, Sefo with four brand-new stitches holding his old thumb onto his old hand. I told him to eat something to build up strength and some new blood cells, but the memory of seeing his own blood cells so eagerly escaping his body and landing on his anticipated dinner earlier made him queasy. He only wanted to lie down.

We gave him until the next day to get some food into

him, and with that came the end of one day of a perfect storm of minor calamities. Two days later I took Sefo back to the hospital to have his wound cleaned and checked and re-bandaged. I helped him find his way back to the hospital because he had only been there that one time, in the dark.

We registered him at the front desk and went to the proper waiting room. The nurse told me I could go because the doctor spoke English and Sefo knew he could now find his way home from here.

On the way out of the hospital, I almost walked right into Illyan. We were both a bit surprised to see each other there, although he knew Sefo was due back at hospital that day to have his hand checked. There was just no way he could have known when, and if he had, he could have gone with Sefo instead of having me do it, so I thought he was there to pick up Sefo, but the thought made no sense.

It turned out that Illyan also needed to see a doctor urgently for some strange protrusion from his chest that had appeared suddenly a short time before. We dug out the emergency phone list to see if one of the three school doctors could see him or whether we needed to go back inside the hospital.

All three doctor's offices were closed due to Fasching, so we did an about face and went straight back inside the hospital and registered another student for emergency and sat down and waited beside Sefo.

In the end, Illyan had an unexplained 'occurrence' but was fine, although for a while it looked like he had a baby's foot sticking out below his rib cage. Sefo went back to eating solid food. And we all survived, but now I keep a first aid kit in my room.

London Calling

The day you buy your plane ticket home from a trip like this is the day you set out on a new path in life. A sort of mental endurance race leaves the starting blocks and doesn't stop until you are seated in your plane on the homeward journey. What will you still have a chance to see in the time left?

This question brings with it an awful feeling of weighty responsibility. How have I done so far? Have I seen enough? Does it justify all that I undertook to get and remain here for the last year? Does this new turning point make me feel better or worse about what I have accomplished? What about the wasted or bad days? Do I wish I could fix them?

I have just booked my return flight home. I came here with a one-way ticket because it was less of a strain on my wallet at the time, but booking the return suddenly landed me in a cleft between the two hard spots of what I had and had not yet seen in Europe.

In fact, plunking down the two sums of what I had and had not seen so far and dividing them by the time I had left gave a very unsatisfactory answer. Booking that ticket really meant I had one foot in the grave of my European adventure. My sojourn here, this grand scheme, now suddenly has a 'best before' date on it, and like a leafy green thing left in the depths of a fridge, it will slowly go bad before my eyes unless I do something about it. I feel a desperate urge to do something with it, no matter what that might be.

I pity the people who come on exchange with normal round-trip tickets already in hand. From the first instant −

even before they arrive – they know exactly where and when their adventure will end. Yet I somehow envy them, too, because from the first moment, they can prepare themselves for what is to come. They have a long period of time to grieve their coming loss and pull themselves together, whereas for me, the shock of knowing a firm return date was suddenly quite emotionally jarring.

I have been here nearly 10 months now, and I have only six weeks left. My mind is racing to figure out what I can still see.

Racing, yes, but not going anywhere. More like locked between gears, stuck in neutral, stuck in a tunnel. What can I do? I am not even planning on going anywhere right now. Why is that? There has been nothing but free time. We experienced teacher illness, transit strikes, and an almost complete lack of interest in school on my part. Even if I started this very instant, there seems to be no way to make a dent in what is still left to discover.

I also want to go home. At the same time, I never want to leave Europe. Things I need to do at home are weighing on my mind (find a career would be one of them). The problem is there are just too many things to do here, and they are so much more appealing than what I am doing now and what I need to do when this trip is over. I need to get refocused on the present, or the very near present and get moving again.

A few days later, I discover a new problem: I am again running out of money. This makes me doubly feel that there is too much left to see. How sad to be here without enough funds to do the place justice.

I walk around with this thought for a few days and then decide that there is nothing to do for it. I must bite the bullet and determine to visit at least a few more cities and museums in the time I have left. I just must do it at the absolute lowest cost per city, or per museum. Whatever money I still have needs to go towards this effort. Who knows when I might get another chance?

In this effort to cram in as much as possible into the least amount of time and money, I started looking at all the important art cities that I could still see and thought furiously about how to reach each of them on the absolute minimum of funds. Let me tell you, when you think of seeing the great cities of Europe, this is not the way you want to be thinking of doing it. Still, they say that planning how you get somewhere is half the fun, so I threw myself into the task with wild abandon.

One of the first things I noticed about this system of travel planning was that I had not been travelling alone up to this point. This would make little difference to the costs, but it made all the difference in the planning, because I had almost always left that up to someone else. I almost always relied on a travel companion to decide and then make arrangements about where we would be going, for how long, and when. How this fact had escaped me for so long, I do not know. Somehow I had gotten to many of the places I had actually wanted to go to simply by hanging around other people, listening to their travels goals, and going with their flow. Now I was planning a trip alone.

I am not a details person. There are so many options to consider when planning travel. Times, dates, package deals, early-bird discounts, day tours, hostels, hotels, or private homes. I quickly found out I hate travel planning. It has never been one of my strengths, and it is always a revelation when you come up against one of your dislikes or weaknesses in life (what else has this whole trip been about?).

I especially find this to be the case when, say, about two thirds of your life are already over. Why are there still so many voids and weaknesses in my personality? Why haven't I been perfected yet so I can be reborn in the next life as a butterfly or whatever and be truly free? The worst part is the nagging question: what makes you think you can do anything to improve these weaknesses now? Haven't you had more than enough time already? I guess the moral is to never give up on improving. We will always be facing down new and old obstacles in trying to be the people our dogs want us to be.

Despite my previous lack of travel planning experience, I was able (in fairly short order) to choose London as one of the closest, most important, most easily reached museum havens that I had not yet been to on this trip. Going there would be a bit of a backward progression, but only in terms of that imaginary Grand Tour I am not even on. Still, I could look at it as if it were the homeward leg of some such tour, where the grand tourist's journey would naturally have found its conclusion, and I could take a look at all of the accumulated art from such a journey, all now nicely on display back home in the old country of Great Britain. After all, the museums and grand manors of England are where all of the amassed souvenirs and trinkets (we now refer to them as 'masterpieces' and 'priceless') collected by all of those intrepid, young Grand Tour travellers ended up.

London also proved to be a great destination purely due to the number of people who were offering car rides to the city from my German home. It is a great city that has a lot going for it, far more than just its art treasures. If you want to go to somewhere artsy but obscure, nobody is willing to give you a car-share to get there. Art just doesn't attract enough motorists. Even flying to London is cheap enough, but that is quite a task of getting yourself to and from a set of airports, twice. Driving is rather more of a downtown-to-downtown business. The only problem with car sharing is that you usually need two drivers: one to take you there and one to bring you back. In my case, I was lucky enough to find a driver who was heading back to Germany at about the same time I planned to return, so I (like in olden days) fit myself into his schedule. This little bit of serendipity made my first foray into individual travel planning an easy business. I could not have been prouder of myself.

Sharing a car ride, especially one that lasts for hours, is also a great way to meet people. At the appointed time, I met up with the driver (Robert, from Poland, but a long-time former resident of London now living in Germany) at the curb outside the post office at the main railway station. Two more people showed up within seconds (both from Luxembourg but strangers to each other, both students headed home from studying in Germany). We all piled into the car and were off.

Like usual on a car share where you are paying the driver to take you somewhere, Robert's car was modern and pristine. It was like a six-year-old Audi someone had just driven off the lot for the first time. Travelling this way is infinitely more comfortable and cleaner than any plane or train. Planes are fairly horrible, and trains are not the Orient Express luxury extravaganza you saw in the movies. Cars can stop along the way pretty much anywhere you like them to or whenever you look motion sick. Your belongings are safely stowed right in sight or near you and are not being gone through by anyone travelling with you or who just happens to board for a moment at some random stop. You know in advance how far everyone is going. This lets you decide whether or not you want to strike up a real conversation with them or just confine things to the weather.

Driving from Germany to London is a four-country jaunt that takes less than a day, something even the most hyperactive package bus tour driver would not attempt. You won't see much along the way, though. Other than the odd vista glimpsed through gaps in the trees, the high-speed roads drivers take to get most quickly from Point A to Point B almost without exception pass through some of the most boring countryside and bleakest habitations that Europe has to offer. Granted, you see as little or less from the seat of a plane or a train, especially if you don't get a window. In a car, every seat is a window seat, and you can even open that window if you want to (planes and modern trains are dangerous places to try this). Back roads are always more scenic, but nobody has time for them, and real Europeans see this kind of authentic stuff every day. They just do it when we are not around and not when they are in a hurry to get somewhere far, far away.

So we sped through Germany (nothing to see there), part of Luxembourg (where we dropped off our two friends at a gas station and filled up on what is purportedly cheaper fuel), and hauled the Audi off at top speed to Belgium (looks exactly like the same forests we saw in Luxembourg, but with a few more and really quite beautiful fields and accompanying farming activity), nipped off a corner of France, and arrived at the ferry at Calais to wait for our ship to Dover.

For the crossing, the ferry companies use monster ships that dock in an odd, half-ferry, half-industrial harbour that has got to be the bleakest thing not actually blown apart in World War II at this location. The highlight of the place is passing through some kind of European Union exit control, immediately followed by some type of British pre-entrance clearance (customs will actually be on the other side of the English Channel). All of this activity makes us feel like we are actually going somewhere.

The ferry is travelling from France to Britain, that much is true, but the entire ship (ship, cars, passengers, staff) is really British. If French people do cross over on holidays or shopping weekends (why would they, though, when everything is cheaper in France?), they must be confined to other ships. This run is all about jolly old England.

The people seem so British, so set in their tweedy ways, it is hard to imagine what they were thinking, going to spend a few days in France in the first place. They would have been complete fish out of water there. Almost universally, the passengers are sartorially challenged, ready for the return of a past century. These are not just French people dressing down in tweeds and otherwise plain, heavy fabrics so that they can save a bit on their drycleaning bills when they go home by tossing these old rags in 'le trash' upon their return. No, these are people who have been wearing the same assortment of clothes for decades. After all of the posturing and posing I have been exposed to in the last year concerning the artful wearing of clothes on the continent, the family lounge area of this ship has the feeling of a frumpy, unaired sitting room with a hint of boiled cabbage in it.

Everyone is dressed in some kind of standard-issue, casual, loose-fitting, but highly insulating assortment of jogging pants and sweater or tweed jacket and cord hose. Everyone could easily trade half of their wardrobe with the person immediately to their right and it would make no difference whatsoever in the appearance of the room as a whole.

How they thought that these things were okay for a trip to France, I will never know. You can't just don the same thing you have been wearing for the past week/year and pop over to France in it for a quick getaway. You will never blend in!

Besides the clothing shenanigans, there are other telltale clues that these people are not from 'Europe' but rather from 'The Isles'. The older men (and here I mean Churchill era) were almost uniformly eccentric, something that seems to go along with the earth that is customarily beneath their feet. Brits, after a certain period in history, didn't get out enough, and the gene pool got stretched pretty thin at one point. Eccentric hair, eccentric bodily tics, twitches, shuffling feet, talking to oneself, unprompted nodding, and a sort of stifled public manner that would see them uneasy within the confines of their own living rooms, were to be seen everywhere.

Maybe I was reading too much into it. If some would have stayed in their cars below decks for the voyage, I might not have noticed, but this was not allowed.

Outside the ship, things looked a bit better. On the other side of the water (we were still in France), England is only a thin slice of land on the horizon, but it constantly grows until it resembles exactly the white cliffs of Dover. When we draw closer, Dover sits there, a quaint little town swallowed up, like the beach at Calais was on the other side, by giant ferry terminals and docks and elevated roadways that serve to funnel ferry traffic into and out of the village so that people never have to stop and visit it.

Once off the boat and through the tangled necktie that is the exit from Dover's docks and Britain's customs check, we are soon in green, rolling, open country. This is exactly what England is supposed to be like, the place where every cow wants to live out its days. But Dover to London is an incredibly short drive, and before you know it, the few houses you saw start to hang out in clumps and then groups and then downright nasty looking gangs, until all green space has been threatened at gunpoint to leave the vicinity. And then you face the real England of today, or at least the urban version of it.

That England is approximately anything built after Henry VIII. It is heartbreakingly dull and proceeds to get duller the further you venture into the sprawl that is London. The neighbourhoods have varying characters, but that doesn't mean the quality of life changes. Behind some facades, there is surely a carefree, happy existence taking place. Behind others, you can't see how that would be possible. You also can't tell why the inhabitants are so content to live with the litter and visual chaos that occurs right outside their graffiti-covered doors.

The areas leading into central London are visually dismal when arriving by car. Graffiti is everywhere and yet it is almost an improvement to everything it covers. Here, graffiti artists serve their highest purpose, hiding the eyesores of cookie-cutter, post-War, Modernist architecture as applied through the lens of poverty and the cheapest building departments known to man.

In London, my driver drops me off at a tube station a good distance from the city centre (driving into London's core is time-consuming, stressful, and expensive), but this is fine with me. I am actually happy to get out of the car for a while, plus I have not yet touched British soil (we drove off the boat and did not stop until now).

I change some money by using my bank card in a tube station cash machine, buy an appropriate train ticket for the length of my stay (a bewildering task for the tourist, given all the various options designed for residents and commuters), and hop on a train headed for the heart of town (or one of its many hearts) at Piccadilly Circus.

In this tourist-clogged part of the city, you experience the least authentic yet most stereotypical introduction to the place. Strangely, after walking around, bathed in tourists hailing from all corners of the globe, my first stop is in front of a mock banana treat stand, where Canadian actor Michael Cerra is promoting a new season of the television show *Arrested Development* outside a local cinema. It was strange, a little like at 'home' in Mannheim, where posters for the local pop radio station often feature nothing more than the names of Canadian musical acts currently dominating its playlist. You never really get away from Canada or Canadians, no matter how thinly we are distributed.

Piccadilly, being full of tourists going every which way at once, reminded me of home in Germany but in a strange way, and it was in complete contrast to the tube station from which I had just emerged. Just as Germans walk in a completely disorderly and disorganized fashion that impedes all forward movement and has you bumping into people determinedly crossing a deserted square but oblivious to the collision course they have set for you, the British walk in such an orderly fashion that you can't fit a farthing between them.

They can walk much faster and with virtually no room to spare, because they all walk in the proper direction, on the proper side of the street, at the proper tempo. That proper tempo, especially around tube station entrances, popular stores, and any pub at all is incredibly fast. I found that, in order to cross two lanes of this streaming humanity that at one point blocked my path, it was necessary for me to first join one stream flowing in the wrong direction, then abruptly turn and wedge myself into the oncoming stream in order to avoid having to cross both. If you see a shop window that you would like to take some little time perusing, you cannot simply put on the brakes or double back. You must take note of the shop's general physical location and do an about-face into the opposing stream of pedestrian traffic in order to get the chance to pass in front of its windows again. If you really want to window shop, the only safe place to do so is from inside the shop.

And so it went. All of this careful walking, and London has nothing if not miles and miles and miles within which to practice. London has too much of everything, really. Inside, outside, in pubs, in tourist attractions, at the free museums. The visitor, even one with tons and tons of time on their hands, has to be selective about what important bits of the place he wants to see or he will wind up living in the city without really noticing the fact.

It is therefore almost surprising to be able to find anything about London that is missing, but in my very short visit, I was able to pinpoint two things that truly weren't there. As my trips are largely focused on visiting art galleries and museums, this is where things lacking most often made their 'presence' felt.

On this trip, what was most notably missing was Vincent van Gogh's ultra-famous (well, one version of it, anyway) painting, *Sunflowers*, from the National Gallery. If you are headed to London to look at art, this is undoubtedly one of the treasures you most hope to see, but when I went to the National Gallery, only a print of the painting hung there. This super end-of-an-era work (Van Gogh painted the best things right at the end of his life) was out on loan to the Van Gogh Museum in Amsterdam, as if they didn't already own enough Van Goghs. Van

Gogh's painting, *Chair*, from 1888, was hung as a consolation prize. Who ever heard of *Chair*?

Another thing missing was the light. London, like my usual former home of Victoria, British Columbia, has a little problem getting itself lit by the sun. Not always, of course, but for a good part of the time. The weather on my trip was almost always great, but when it was cloudy or variable or when the sun was partly obscured, the unlit galleries of the National Gallery would darken and lighten as if some over-caffeinated kid was hiding somewhere, monkeying with the dimmer switch.

I can't list it as a lack, but public galleries and museums in Britain do lack an entrance fee, which is a real boon for the visitor in a town where most things are outrageously expensive, especially on a student budget. So in that way, it is really something Britain *has* that most other places don't.

Another thing it had, that almost all other cities on my trip so far had lacked, was artists sketching or copying the paintings in the galleries and museums. This activity always seemed to be part of museum or gallery life in my earlier visits to important collections, but in London, I suddenly realized I had not seen anyone making art in any other museum recently. One of the first ones I saw was copying Paul Delaroche's (1795-1856) *The Execution of Lady Jane Grey*, from 1833. Lady Jane, the title card explained, had been Queen for nine days before she was deposed by the Catholic Queen Mary, of shipping fame. Lady Jane, not so much remembered as Mary, was beheaded at Tower Hill early the following year, aged 17. (And you say you don't know what to do when your kids are misbehaving.) Anyhow, French painter Delaroche was famous for his depictions of British royalty, preferably (and this probably a nod to his own nationalistic sentiments, as well as to those of the British patrons who wanted such paintings) when said royalty was in a bad way, usually either doomed or dying.

Also hanging in the National Gallery is Hans Holbein

the Younger's *The Ambassadors*, from 1533. This masterpiece is surely one of my favourite paintings and shows two youngish French 'diplomats' (only one was) in England at the time of King Henry VIII.

The painting is, in Holbein's usual way, hyper-realistic. Every square inch of the thing (and there are many, many square inches of the thing) is indeed made of paint but seems to have been applied by God-knows-what magic brush, for it all looks absolutely real.

The painting nearly seems photographed, except for the weird, continually changing perspective, as if each important feature of the painting (a face, a hand, a globe of the earth) had been closely scrutinized on its own and then painted into the appropriate place. Each object seems looked at from dead centre and then copied to the canvas from that viewpoint.

Overall, though, it is perfection. If you study art from the angle of beauty or just sheer level of technical skill or faithfulness to the scene, this is the man you want to go see. Holbein's painting, *The Schutzmantel Madonna* (it goes by a host of other names) from just slightly earlier, features the mother of Christ protecting the former Mayor of Basel, Switzerland, and his family (including his dead wife and an unidentified child). It is similarly perfect in all of its individual details and very near photographic except when all of its features are viewed together, due to that shifting perspective.

But *The Ambassadors* has something more. Stretched out along a good portion of the lower foreground of the painting is a grey and black blob. It looks like a smeary accident some careless assistant made and then tried to clean up before the master returned, but that is not what it is. We now know that the blob was meant to be there, despite appearing entirely out of place, floating above the elaborate floor (it even casts its own shadow) of this otherwise photographic image. If you step over to the extreme right side of the painting and look back along its surface, you will see that the blob transforms into a human skull. You need to get as close to the picture plane as possible, but the security guards allow you to do this and no alarm is triggered.

The question you have to ask yourself is, what is this thing doing here in an otherwise realistic rendering of two men standing either side of a shelf full of scientific and religious objects, all rendered in absolute realistic perfection? The distorted skull casually floats above the floor, stretched out so as to be unrecognizable from the front of the painting (viewed head on, it resembles a floating, dried up fish skeleton). The shadow the skull casts falls in the *opposite* direction to all other shadows in the picture.

What was Holbein trying to say by including it? That the young subjects of his painting, no matter how youthful and rich now, had better watch out in the future? That when the bell tolls, it tolls for everybody, sometimes all at once? The subjects of the painting, clearly in their glory days, were also the patrons of the painting. Did they really want to be thusly reminded that they too one day would be gone, no more than ashes and dust? If so, why did they choose such a strange way to do it? Half-hidden and yet obvious, right there in your face, staring back at you. Holbein was obviously on board with the idea and may have been the originator of it.

It is a strange puzzle. The painter was equally young and rich and famous. He didn't need to put up with any strange ideas from his clients. He was a superstar who travelled from his home in Switzerland (he was born in Germany, or what would today be in Germany) to paint the rich and famous of London and King Henry's court. Yet foreigners like these two Frenchmen in *The Ambassadors* gave him his best commissions.

Maybe he did just paint what they wanted after all, but the skull doesn't seem to fit the painting or Holbein's previous track record of being perhaps overly faithful to realism if not reality (he freely introduced or rearranged things in his paintings).

The history of painting in England is so long and rich, it just reminds you of how wealthy and powerful the British once were. To think I will only be visiting London! Imagine all the other art that is in every single other large city or town or country house in the land. It boggles the mind. The things these people bought, picked up, stole, looted, plundered, and otherwise brought back home, from all around the world, are stunning, in sheer numbers and in quality.

Add to that the ability of that ruling class to attract, at any given time, the greatest talents the world had to offer for making luxury items such as paintings, sculptures, jewelry, or even furniture, and you come to a staggering conclusion: Britain used to be made of money.

You can still see some of the money – and some of Britain's wide-reaching world influence, especially in economics – if you take a stroll through the part of town known as The City, which you certainly do it you are on an art and architectural tour of London.

The City is the few golden blocks of real estate north of the Thames and across the river from the Tate Modern museum. It is the financial heart of London. You can visit it on the walk back from the Tate or after viewing Christopher Wren's St. Paul's Cathedral. I could go on and on about the Tate or St. Paul's or Wren or his massive influence on the city and the history of architecture, but walking through the site of so much financial business really keeps your mind on the money.

Not far from St. Paul's is the perfect reminder of all this. It is Suttons & Robertsons, 'Pawnbrokers of Distinction, since 1770'. This establishment is in operation today on Fleet Street at the corner of St. Bride's Avenue, if you happen to be in need of it.

Its presence in the heart of the financial district reminds you that, yes, this city was built on money, and that money also oiled the machine that is the art world, and that people here made money and spent money, sometimes freely and lavishly, on such luxuries as portraits or pretty pictures of bits of countryside yet to be ruined by Industrial Revolution.

But a pawnbroker is a reminder that things don't work out for everybody, not always. Suttons & Robertsons have been pawnbrokering – distinctively – for longer than Britain has been a superpower. Even Britain, in a sense, didn't 'make it'.

The sign at Suttons & Robertsons says, 'Discreet and trusted for over 200 years' and, if you happen to be wondering how helpful a pawnbroker can be in an extremely ritzy city, the sign that adds 'Loans of up to 1 million Pounds' should help put that into perspective. What do you think people can pawn for which they will receive 1 millions Pounds? Hmm?

This city, which represented an empire, this city which was about making money and wielding power and rewarding itself with baubles, has taken its chances and seen good times and bad. It is the home of the all-in Lloyds of London insurance company, the only one most people know that actually took chances. There are more minor nobles here collecting art than you can shake a stick at. But sometimes the mighty fall. People like Suttons & Robertsons are there to help them get back up again, for a small fee.

The two subjects of Holbein's *The Ambassadors* both came from wealthy and powerful French families with long pedigrees that are now far past their primes and virtually forgotten. Things come about, as they often do, through a combination of things: not producing heirs, the French Revolution, incurable diseases of the time.

There are good life lessons in the painting for a person like me who is a little late getting started on a particular path. Who knew that I would feel the weight of this so strongly from just a few days in London, a spot I wasn't even intending to visit on this Grand Tour?

But I did, and I had no small amount of time in which to reflect upon it. I was alone on this trip, one of the few times I have ever been alone anywhere. And I learned, in just a few days of wandering around seeing the art and architecture and the traces of the money that bought it all, that not everybody makes it, and nobody makes it forever.

London is a melting pot, as is the wider world out there. Some people bob to the surface no matter what originally pushed them down, but most just remain part of the liquid mass that holds the few aloft.

Maybe it is okay to just be happy that we are all in one big, warm pot together. Maybe. At least for now.

Odds and Ends

Not every event that takes place during my exchange year has to fit into a larger story or offer a bigger, more meaningful message, does it? They could, but I haven't in all cases found that place. I haven't even put all of the stories in order. Still, I don't want you to go home without them, so here they are, in no particular order, other than that in which I remember them.

I once had to pick up five Egyptian girls from the train station and take them back to their new dorm. This wouldn't normally have been such a big problem, but when they finally arrived and found me waiting for them at the appointed place, it immediately became clear just how big of a problem the task was going to be.

These five girls, between them, seemed to have smuggled all of the luggage off of their plane. I imagined stunned guests somewhere in an airport terminal standing hypnotized by a spinning, empty baggage carousel.

I have no idea how these girls were able to get all of that luggage onto their plane, let alone past customs, onto the train, and then before my waiting eyes, but they kindly explained how they had gotten it all to fly, then shifted it from terminal to train, then back down to the platform and onto terra firma before me. That required helping each other use trunks to jam open automatic doors, carefully reading the loading capacity of elevators, monopolizing escalators and stairwells, then using a human chain to slide the bags forward to the very spot where I was standing.

It was clear that we would not be able to get on either the bus or the streetcar with this overloaded circus. There was a veritable herd of luggage drooping tiredly around us. You only had so much time to get on, get organized within, and then get off a bus or streetcar. No bus or streetcar driver would put up with such a delay. Any passengers already on the bus or streetcar would be squeezed out the other doors like toothpaste and into oblivion. There would be no room inside the vehicle for air. We would have produced a blockage like an ostrich egg in a garter snake.

As I might have mentioned elsewhere, students also have little money available to them at any one time, no matter how much they might spend over the course of their exchange. And some solutions are just too expensive for them. They prefer to save wherever they can, but sometimes (this would be one of them) they have to bight the bullet and dig into their wallets or purses. It looked like we would need to take five taxis to get all of these students and their chattels the fifteen long blocks to home.

I took a scouting party to the taxi stand outside the train station while the other students stayed behind to calm the luggage so it didn't scatter. Until this point, I had never taken a cab in Germany and was unsure of their rates. I had just always avoided them as being needlessly expensive. I was pleasantly surprised to see a number of minivans serving as taxis. This would help bring down our total number of units needed. Things were potentially looking up.

As everyone knows, though, taxi stands are complicated affairs with unposted rules and an invisible hierarchy between the drivers and their companies and who came first and so on. And we immediately ran afoul of this system by going up and talking to a driver who, to our eyes, seemed to be at the head of the line but was not.

He managed to get a van driver from among the large group of drivers (who were berating us with the unpublished rules) to pull out of line and whip around in front of all these others (he was the next van in line, and this was fine with everybody, it turned out). Other waiting drivers, farther away and not part of our melee, honked and complained at this, but the elders we had gathered sanctioned the move, so there was nothing they could do. How could those other drivers help us with our Mt. Everest of luggage, anyway? They couldn't without a van, so they sat around and sulked or got out of their cars and came over to watch the show we were about to put on.

The driver of the van (I wish he had been Egyptian or at least Arabic speaking, which could have made things go a whole lot better) thought he could help us and started stuffing the luggage into his vehicle. This was not easy. Most pieces were seriously oversized and overweight, and he had a big job.

A few minutes later, his van was stuffed full of luggage, and the cracks in this system began to appear. There was no room for any passengers, and there were still five pieces of luggage on the pavement. That makes five Egyptian girls, five bags, and myself still on the ground. This is not bad, considering I first thought we would require five taxis to move this load, but it was clear that one minivan was not going to cut it.

The driver wanted to get the address of the destination, then drive the luggage there while we all climbed into another van – hopefully with the remaining luggage – or hopped on the next passing bus or streetcar. For his part, he wanted 20 Euros.

The part I didn't like was the security level. What school of taxi driving had this guy gone to back in his home country? Didn't he know the world-famous scam of leaving your luggage with a stranger? Travellers to places such as Mexico have been telling this story since the beginning of time: people hitch rides with passing drivers and just need to duck into the next toilet only to emerge to no driver, no car, no luggage. It is a classic tale.

This was just an overall bad idea, really, although the driver seemed sincere, and we probably could have followed him pretty closely in a series of other minivans, if need be. But just then, another van driver standing around watching the progress spoke up that a taxi driver could only charge a set rate per bag for luggage in Mannheim, and the total fare would be very low unless he took some passengers.

Our loaded driver took offence at this revelation, but the second driver stood by the rule, and other drivers shook their heads in agreement. It made no sense – according to the rules – if a taxi didn't also carry some passengers, this second driver said. He had obviously learned his art at a better taxi driving school.

The whole direction of this conversation had tipped our first driver into his red zone, and he was done with us. He wasn't taking luggage, he wasn't taking passengers, he wasn't taking a little bit of each. He was booking off for the night.

He pulled all of the luggage out of the van, and the second driver went over and brought his own van around, stuffed all the luggage inside – and I mean all of the luggage, including the five wayward pieces – and got all five Egyptian girls and myself onto seats and drove off. I couldn't believe it; it was approximately the same minivan. At the other end, things went just as smoothly, and the bill was exactly the same 20 Euro standard fare.

The start of the second semester was a bit rocky in that way. I once had to pick up a set of twins from the train station and had noted that they were coming at midnight on a certain day. In fact, they were coming at midnight of the previous day, there being a sort of 'midnight' that occurs at about 12:01 a.m. on a Friday, let's say, and then another 'midnight' about 24 hours later, at 11:59 p.m. on the very same Friday. Are you with me?

I thought they were coming at the *end* of a certain day, when actually they came right at the very *beginning* of that day, 24 hours less a minute earlier than I was planning.

When they called my phone one entire day ahead of schedule and in the middle of the night, I was perplexed, not least because I had just fallen asleep after a lengthy kitchen party. The girls on the other end of the phone were equally perplexed that I was not there to meet them. I told them I would get there as soon as possible.

As you have learned, the streetcar and bus frequency at this hour is deplorable. It would be better to ride my bike from the dorm to the train station, then lock and leave it there while I brought the twins back to the dorm, rather than endure the lengthy wait and slow ride the public transport system would require. But when I went to get my bike, I discovered its taillight was not working. This happens often enough (the tiny bulbs are fragile and endure a lot of bouncing), but I was really hoping to tear through town in the dark and didn't want the distraction of worrying about the police stopping me. But would could I do? The twins had already been waiting at the train station for some time before they phoned, so I headed out in full contravention of the rather sticky German bicycle laws and hoped for the best.

Once again in this trip, I was learning to bend or break rules and not worry so much about the little things. If I got stopped, I got stopped and could talk and talk and explain myself, and if I received a ticket or was told to push the bike the rest of the way, well, I would deal with it then. (I would push the bike around the next corner before hopping on and riding the rest of the way to the train station. So there.)

Still, being late, missing appointments, and breaking laws makes me nervous, so I was wide awake and a little agitated when I pulled up and found the girls. And there was more. Not only did I not yet have the keys to their rooms (nobody was supposed to move in until 9 a.m. that morning, part of the reason I believed the girls were arriving at the midnight that was *after* the morning, the midnight that was yet to come), but there were two sets of twins instead of just one.

What was going on here? I was tired, it was late, I was a

little disoriented, but it turned out I was picking up three new students: one set of twins and half of a second set of twins. The spare twin was just travelling with the others, all best friends for life, and would be continuing on a solo journey in a few days. But for now, not only did I have two extra twins on my hands, I had absolutely nowhere to put them until morning.

With the bus and streetcar running only once an hour at this point, we did not even reach the dorm until well past 3 a.m. And all we could do was go up to my empty kitchen and get them somewhat settled there. The girls said they planned to stay up and chat on their phones with family and friends back home and that they would probably not sleep at all, due to excitement, and for a while, they probably didn't.

As the kitchen was directly across the hall from my door, I told them to come see me any time they needed something or had a question. I felt sorry that I couldn't offer them more than coffee and tea and the promise to get their room keys first thing in the morning, as planned. They didn't seem to need me hanging around, so I went back to my own bed. There was no room in my place for much more than one twin at a time, which didn't seem fair, so I left them all to themselves and fell asleep.

They did not come by to ask for anything during the morning hours, and when I woke, I went to check on them. They were all still in the kitchen, but they made the strangest, saddest sight: the four twins were all asleep, most of them on piles of clothes that they had heaped up into makeshift mattresses inside their open suitcases. One was sitting in a chair with her head on the table. I guess they had gotten so tired that they eventually needed sleep and had to curl up in the tiny beds of their open suitcases.

Now I felt worse than ever and tried to do whatever I could to make it up to them during their stay. We got the keys from the Hausmeister and settled the girls in their new rooms. The extra sister stayed a few days, and then went away. I helped everybody get proper Internet connections (always a challenge here), and so on. For the rest of the semester, one of the twins (when I did something useful) would say, "I love you, Bryce" and then, just as heartily (when I did something wrong) say, "I hate you, Bryce." We travelled together a bit and went to many events, and she never failed to say one or the other of those things to me on a daily basis. Sometimes she said both.

That reminds me of the Madonna of Dresden. I had gone to that city on a school trip and museum tour, mostly to see Raphael's *Sistine Madonna* on display there. For many art lovers, it is the single biggest draw of the city's art world. The 1512 painting is partly so famous and endearing because it features two delightful cherubs who lounge around the lower edge of the frame and have been reproduced millions and millions of times on everything from packaging to advertising to greeting cards. You might not know whence they come, but you know the ones I mean. Oh, and the painting has been called 'supreme' and 'divine.'

It hangs in the Old Masters gallery in Dresden, and it is one of the world's art must sees. It is massive, mounted at the end of a long gallery, and a crowd usually builds in front of it, similar to the one that goes to gaze in wonder at the *Mona Lisa*.

Like all large Old Masters galleries, this one takes either hours or days to properly make your way through, but everyone who has even five minutes will go to see the *Madonna* at the end of her special room. Every guided tour dutifully files past it.

I had already seen her and was on my way out of the gallery after hours and hours spent there when I passed a tour group of women coming up the main staircase, headed for the *Madonna*. I had seen many tour groups already that day, but something struck me about this one, because I had never seen a tour group made up only of women before.

As that thought was running through my mind, a member of the group passed close to me on the stairs and fairly locked eyes with me as she went by. That doesn't happen often. It was a grand staircase. It was a grand stare, and she was on her way to see a grand painting. Something about the moment was simply grand. I don't know why I couldn't stop myself, but I stared back as she passed and then a few stairs later, I turned around to see her go the rest of the way up the staircase. She was still looking back at me.

Apart from her slightly longer, curlier, more orange hair, she looked a lot like Raphael's *Madonna*, except she was part of a packaged tour and was about 500 years younger. This is hard to put across properly, but despite the gulf between whatever lives we lived at that moment, what languages we spoke, our cultures or circumstances (I heard something like Polish coming out of her tour guide) art had, for that moment, brought us together.

If you asked me to draw her face today, I could not, not because I can't draw, but because I can't remember what it looked like. Now I just like to think of her as the true Dresden Madonna and hope that she is still out there somewhere, drinking in the sights in other Old Masters galleries on a packaged tour somewhere.

Epilogue

And now, by some strange twist of fate, here I am again. Three months after having left Germany for Canada, I am back in Europe. This time, I might be here for a long, long time.

This is not what I was expecting, not what was supposed to happen. Despite my lack of planning as to what I would do when I got back to Canada, I was still fully expecting to live there after this exchange. I would have eventually found something to do within my new chosen field. My interlude living my European dream was meant to be just that: an interlude, a dream. Now it was supposed to be over.

This whole book has been leading up to that ending (there was never supposed to be an epilogue). This tale was meant to chronicle the once-in-a-lifetime adventure of going overseas as an international exchange student for my final year of university at the tender age of 48. Well, that was the plan, except that now the year has ended, but the book and the European dream have not. Believe me, I am as shocked as you are.

Now, here I sit, typing these words at my new kitchen table in my new girlfriend's apartment, back in Mannheim, writing what was never meant to be. In one fell swoop, my finishing year has become less of the one-shot deal of *A Year in Provence* and more of the consecutive summers of *Under the Tuscan Sun*, albeit with less cooking. And that is fine with me: bring on the Europe. Some people can't seem to get enough of the place. I might once again be one of them.

This time around, although I have only been back for a

few days, everything is different. I already know the streets. I still have my old phone number and bank account. There will be no awkward phase of getting to know the most basic routines in order to sustain everyday life. No paranoid-schizophrenic is going to corner me in front of the train station this time for a long chat on the pros and cons of the Illuminati. And I have already discovered, through much personal exertion and dogged determination, which street-side seller makes the best Döner in the city.

I am not a student on exchange here anymore, either. Now I *live* here, and instead of my tiny student dorm, we share (thanks to that girlfriend) a normal (and comfortable) downtown flat. Although I am still writing my book with the aid of an old, manual typewriter, even the typewriter has been changed (I foolishly took my previous one home, then spent the first few days back here finding an exact replica with the same wonderfully smooth operation of the original).

The biggest change, though, is that I am no longer alone. I will not go forward in this life as a bachelor (I thought I might). I probably won't settle in Canada, at least for some time. This country and this language and then, in the larger sense, this continent full of art are going to grow on me and be part of every breath I take going forward. And so will the girl.

This changes everything: how I will go about a job search, and what exactly I will do in this industry, and with whom.

One thing remains the same: I am still studying. I still need two more courses in order to finish my degree. I will take one online from my home university and the other the way I took my earlier art courses here, with a few professor meetings and a whole lot of independent study and museum visits. But I no longer live the life of a student.

That means I won't meet the new crop of students, or not often anyway, and the old students I once knew have now mostly moved on (Jose and Iris, from Taiwan, remain, while a few others plan to come back for a semester or a visit, whichever suits their plans).

My dorm room is now a distant memory, its austere, prison-like demeanour largely forgotten, as is the prison across the street from it. I find it ironic when Jose tells me that a neighbourhood drug dealer has now taken up residence in one of the dorm's kitchens in order to better serve his school- and university-age clientele. It is absolutely the most fitting and yet unlikeliest place from which to run a broad-daylight drug supply enterprise.

There is a bit more road to travel before I have my honours degree in art history, and it has been a long road. Without the distraction and sensations this final year in Europe has brought – as well as the financial support, however small – I do not know if I would be this close to the end of that road. I can say unequivocally that I am tired of studying, tired of being a student, and that I regularly daydream about not having to study any more. But I also regularly browse art world courses, to see what might be next for me, and my eye has been fairly captured by a master's program in nearby Heidelberg that passes one year there and one year at the Louvre in Paris for a specialization in museology. It seems too interesting to be true.

I can almost but not quite picture myself doing it, wasting another two years of my life on that adventure. Almost. Studying, as the Immortal Bard might have said, is such sweet sorrow.

No matter what I do, for now at least, I can't seem to get away from school or its impact. Almost three years ago, I decided to go back to school to finish my degree, partly to show myself and my two sons that higher education is worth the effort and to finish things we start. At that time, one of my boys had already dropped out of high school and the other one seemed to be struggling with the idea of finishing. Both are doing fine, the bigger one driving around in my old Porsche and managing a large clothing store, and the smaller one working on becoming a manager for the same clothing store chain, but with a high school diploma in his hand.

So now there is nobody left to prove anything to except myself. Two courses from now, I guess I will also be convinced.

Despite still being a hair's breadth away from having my degree, I can teach a course or two here at my old university to pass the school year before we go to Canada in summer for an initial inspection tour (the girl has never been there) and to start to build the house that – two years ago – I poured a foundation for on Prince Edward Island. We are looking forward to it: the space of a real house, yard, and garden (all things we do not have here) on our farm that is just standing still and empty, waiting for us.

Life here is already much better than my former student days. Now, we enjoy a two-bedroom apartment where one bedroom serves as a writing room and office. The location couldn't be better. I have just come back from the market in the city centre, blocks away, where I love to go but never shopped as a student (it can be slightly more expensive than grocery stores). I have just bought new wine from the neighbouring Pfalz region, famous for its vineyards. We will take these bottles (entirely sweet and with only slightly more alcohol than grape juice) as a gift for the girlfriend's parents when we visit them tomorrow in the village where her father was raised.

All in all, we are nesting nicely. In the next few months, we will buy a new printer, a car, a television, a Weimaraner puppy, and some things for the kitchen. The girlfriend cooks wonderfully and loves doing it, and the tiny kitchen here is too small for us to both occupy at the same time. What could be better than that? We will build a bigger kitchen in PEI so that I can at least chop vegetables, but for now, I am largely off the hook in culinary matters.

I did not think at the beginning of all of this that I

would ever be back in this city. The world is too big of a place for that. There is so much left to see, but like any good place, this one grows on you, and part of its appeal is the company you keep. My school friends are gone, but the girlfriend is here, there is work to do, plans to make, and her circle of friends to meet, so life can be complete.

Despite my daydreaming about further degrees, my school days will likely soon end. I will go on to other things, possibly dealing in art (can there be a better place?) or something (God forbid) completely unrelated. There might still be a career somewhere out there on my horizon.

Somehow we will do something. It might be here; it might be back in Canada (where hopefully we will always spend some part of every year). With luck, we will end up passing a lot of time in the freedom of our farm space, attending to our pastimes: tinkering with old cars (me), cooking (her), gardening (us). Maybe we will start a new family, to keep that dog busy. And maybe we will get the time to finish some other long-delayed projects.

But those would be other stories for other books.

About *Finishing Year*

Can a man change his stars? Can he ever really rise above? These are the questions that plague our mortal souls. Bryce Finley, a 48-year-old Canadian single father with an unfinished university degree, two nearly grown children, and no visible (future) means of support, is about to find out.

After three years working at his local university, he decides to hit the books and go back to finish his degree and show his kids he never meant to be a dropout. His eldest has already quit high school, but is there still time to show the youngest one?

When his university contract ends, completing his long-delayed education in art history proves to be financially difficult, so he jumps at the chance to study – with the aid of a small scholarship – as an international exchange student in Europe.

What follows is a life in a cramped student dorm in an industrial town in Germany that is – luckily – an ideal jumping off point for visiting the great art capitals of Europe.

Life-changing experiences follow, along with chances to reflect and improve upon a life some have called "a financial train wreck," in which only one of his two kids might ever graduate from high school, and in which our hero finally realizes he never, ever, decided what to be when he grew up.

But that was then, this is now, and class is in session. With style, humour, and cunning linguistics, Finley makes his way through his last year of university, the great museums of Europe, and the social fabrics of a handful of European countries, to emerge a wiser, more educated, and potentially more employable person.

About the author

Bryce Finley, a former journalist and photographer, is the author of four previous books, and a potential future art dealer, or something.

35661652R00146

Made in the USA
Charleston, SC
15 November 2014